Sexual Harassment:
Your Guide to Legal Action

What You Should Know
and
What You Can Do

Sexual Harassment: Your Guide to Legal Action

What You Should Know
and
What You Can Do

Mary L. Boland
Attorney at Law

SPHINX® PUBLISHING
AN IMPRINT OF SOURCEBOOKS, INC.®
NAPERVILLE, ILLINOIS
www.SphinxLegal.com

First Edition, 2002

Published by: **Sphinx® Publishing, An Imprint of Sourcebooks, Inc.®**

Naperville Office
P.O. Box 4410
Naperville, Illinois 60567-4410
630-961-3900
Fax: 630-961-2168
www.sourcebooks.com
www.SphinxLegal.com

This publication is designed to provide accurate and authoritative information in regard to the subject matter covered. It is sold with the understanding that the publisher is not engaged in rendering legal, accounting, or other professional service. If legal advice or other expert assistance is required, the services of a competent professional person should be sought.

From a Declaration of Principles Jointly Adopted by a Committee of the American Bar Association and a Committee of Publishers and Associations

This product is not a substitute for legal advice.

Disclaimer required by Texas statutes.

Library of Congress Cataloging-in-Publication Data

Boland, Mary L.
    Sexual harassment : your guide to legal action : what you should know and what you can do / Mary L. Boland.-- 1st ed.
        p. cm.
    Includes index.
    ISBN 1-57248-217-6 (alk. paper)
    1. Sexual harassment--Law and legislation--United States--Popular works. I. Title.

KF4758.Z9 B65 2002
344.7301'4133--dc21

2002026678

Printed and bound in the United States of America.

VHG Paperback — 10 9 8 7 6 5 4 3 2 1

CONTENTS

YOU ARE
NOT ALONE

"A...student should feel safe and comfortable walking down the halls of his or her school. School is a place for learning and growing. Sexual harassment stops that process." *Department of Education, Office for Civil Rights pamphlet, "Sexual Harassment: It's not Academic"* citing to Stein, N. & Sjostram, Lisa, *Flirting or Hurting? A Teacher's Guide on Student to Student Sexual Harassment in Schools* 66 (Washington, D.C.: NEA Professional Library Publication, 1994).

"A work environment consumed by remarks that intimidate, ridicule, and maliciously demean the status of women can create an environment that is as hostile as an environment that contains unwanted sexual advances." *Smith v. First Union National Bank,* 202 F. 3d 234, 242 (4th Cir. 2000)

Equal treatment at school and work is a civil right under federal and state laws. Sexual harassment is a type of sex discrimination involving unwelcome sexual conduct or pressure in school or the workplace. The laws say that no one should have to attend school or work in a "locker room" type atmosphere, and no one has the right to sexually bully another person at school or work. The laws apply to either sex, and both men and women can be harassers or harassed. However, overwhelmingly, sexual harassment is a form of discrimination practiced by men and boys against women and girls.

How Often Sexual Harassment Occurs

Sexual harassment is an immense problem at school and in the workplace. Every year tens of thousands of females and several thousand males come forward to report their experiences to their schools, employers, federal and state agencies. A few file lawsuits to recover their losses.

In Schools

In the late 1980's, the American Association of University Women conducted the first scientific survey of high schoolers. In all, they questioned more than 1600 teenagers in grades 8-11 about sexual harassment in school. Their report, called "Hostile Hallways," produced shocking numbers: 85% of the girls and 76% of the boys reported sexual harassment. (See Bryant, A. "Hostile Hallways: The AAUW survey on Sexual Harassment in America's Schools," J. of School Health No. 63, pp355-57 (1993) (reporting statistics on the AAUW survey).) The high rate of sexual harassment reported by these teens has been confirmed by later surveys.

Perhaps more disturbing is that sexual harassment begins much earlier than high school. In fact, children in the third grade have reported being targeted for sexual harassment. Sometimes, the harassment starts even earlier.

CASE

A six year old complained that a group of boys on her bus repeatedly used profanity, called her obscene names, referred to her genitalia, and suggested that she perform oral sex on her father. (See Amy Saltzman, "It's Not Just Teasing," U.S. NEWS & WORLD REP., Dec. 6, 1993, at 73.)

Furthermore, sexual harassment increasingly becomes more common as students move through elementary and high school. In various studies, 6% of third graders, 30% of sixth graders, and 80% of teens have reported being sexually harassed in schools.

> An 8th grader complained to her school that several boys began repeatedly mocking her in the halls and on the bus, yelling "Moo moo" and making vulgar references to her breasts and other parts of her body. (See Margaret Lillard, "Boys Will Be Boys? No More Say Schoolgirls, Fed Up With Harassment," AP (May 31, 1993).)

CASE

The number of students who are sexually harassed is also high in college-aged students. 67% of female students and 15% of male students have reported sexual harassment. (See Katie Herrick & Jamilla Coleman, "Campus Confidential," Glamour Magazine, Sept. 9, 1999, at 190 and Sarah K. Murnen & Linda Smolak, "The Experience of Sexual Harassment Among Grade-School Students: Early Socialization of Female Subordination?" Sex Roles: Journal of Research (July 2000).)

> "Dr. P. gave me the creeps. Whenever we took a test, I'd look up from my paper, and there he would be staring at me. He was always looking at my top or my legs. I quit wearing skirts to that class because I was so uncomfortable around him. I felt like I was some kind of freak in a zoo." (Excerpt from Ivory Power: Sexual Harassment on Campus, ed. Michele Paludi p.6. (Reporting a results from a campus study by Dziech and Weiner in 1984).) (See Hughes, Jean O'Gorman and Bernice R. Sandler, Peer Harassment: Hassles for Women on Campus, Center for Women Policy Studies, Washington DC (1988).)

CASE

In the Workplace

Sexual harassment is also a severe problem in the workplace. In the 1970s, researchers estimated that as many as one out of every two women would become a victim of sexual harassment in her work environment.

But in the first survey of sexual harassment in the workplace, the numbers proved much higher. When *Redbook Magazine* asked readers whether they had experienced sexual harassment, about 9,000 women responded. Nearly nine out of ten of the women reported that they had been targets of sexual harassment in their workplaces. (See C. Safran, "What Men Do To Women On the Job," Redbook Magazine (Nov. 1976)(reader questionnaire).)

Other surveys taken around that time produced equally high percentages, showing that between 50-70% of women had been sexually harassed at work. For example, the Redbook article reports a random survey conducted by a naval officer who used the same questionnaire to poll women on his base and in a nearby town in California. In that poll, 81% of the women said they had experienced sexual harassment. A Cornell University survey also found that 70% of the respondents had experienced sexual harassment.

A 1992 survey in *Working Woman* magazine of over 9,000 readers showed that more than 60% of the women reported being harassed, and more than a third knew a co-worker who had been harassed. (See R. Sandroff, "Sexual Harassment: The Inside Story," Working Woman, p. 47 (June 1992).)

The federal government has also documented a high rate of sexual harassment of the federal workforce. The U.S. Merit Systems Protection Board conducted a series of studies of sexual harassment in the federal government workforce in 1981, 1987 and 1994. (See U.S. Merit Systems Protection Board, Sexual Harassment of Federal Workers: Is it a Problem? Washington, D.C.: U.S. Gov't Printing Office (1981); U.S.

Merit Systems Protection Board, Sexual Harassment of Federal Workers: An Update. Washington, D.C.: U.S.Gov't Printing Office (1987); and. U.S. Merit Systems Protection Board, Sexual Harassment in the Federal Workplace: Trends, Progress, Continuing Challenges. Washington, D.C.: U.S. Gov't Printing Office (1994).) These surveys, taken of thousands of federal workers, showed that around 42% of women in 1981 and 1987, and 44% in 1994 reported being sexually harassed on the job.

The numbers of workers who complain of sexual harassment in the private and public workforces also remain high. Employment discrimination complaints have tripled during the past decade. In fact, sexual harassment is now the basis for a third of all harassment claims handled by the federal agency charged with investigating sexual harassment in the workplace, and complaints of school-based sexual harassment continue to increase.

THE COST OF SEXUAL HARASSMENT

Sexual harassment is very costly. Lost career and educational opportunities are difficult to measure, but statistics can tell part of the story. By the end of the 1980s, more than 90% of large companies reported cases and 40% of large companies had been sued for sexual harassment. (See Klein Assoc., Inc., The 1988 Working Women Sexual Harassment Survey Executive Report, Klein Associates, Inc. Cambridge, MA (1988).) During a two-year period in the mid-1990s, sexual harassment cost the federal government (and us as taxpayers) more than 300 million dollars. The U.S. Department of Labor estimates that private businesses lose around $1 billion annually due to sexual harassment. This figure does not include the millions of dollars of judgment awards in sexual harassment cases every year. For example, over $150 million was awarded to victims in sexual harassment lawsuits in 1999. Many large school districts spend over $1 million annually to train staff and students on sexual harassment issues as they try to avoid the expense of potential lawsuits. In California alone in 1999, it was estimated that school districts representing half the students in the state paid out $80 million dollars in tort-related litigation in one year. (See John Wilson, "Local Government Liability: A Major Cost and Exposure," Cal. Tax Digest, (February 1999).)

INTRODUCTION

Every year in this country, sexual harassment costs hundreds of millions of dollars in lost educational and job opportunities, mostly for girls and women who are likely to be sexually harassed at school or at work during their lives.

A zero tolerance policy for sexual harassment is needed. Until recently, the law treated sexual harassment as a "personal problem" in the workplace. It wasn't even an issue for schools. For workers, it was Anita Hill's testimony before Congress in 1991 that opened the doors of justice to the tens of thousands of women and several thousand men who came forward to complain of sexual harassment. Schools became sensitive to sexual harassment after the U.S. Supreme Court said that they could be sued for money damages discussed in Chapter 11. Even with increased sensitivity, complaints of sexual harassment in schools and workplaces have continued to climb in the last decade, more than tripling according to federal statistics.

The goal of this book is to make you aware of your right to be free of sexual harassment at work and school. You will gain some self-help preventive and responsive strategies to deal with sexually harassing situations in Chapters 5, 9, 10, 13, and 14. You will learn what your school or employer is (or should be) doing about it and where to turn for assistance in Chapters 5, 7, and 12. You will learn how to make a complaint of sexual harassment and understand how it is investigated by federal and state agencies in Chapter 10. This book will also provide you with the resource information to enable you to consider filing a civil lawsuit to recover your losses. The glossary will help you with many of the legal terms used in this book, while the appendices will give you specific laws and resources.

SECTION ONE:

Overview of Sexual Harassment

WHAT SEXUAL HARASSMENT IS

1

Sexually obnoxious behavior involves a range of conduct from minor offensive words or acts to forced sexual activity and even rape. Not all of this type of conduct will be considered severe enough to form the basis for a legal claim of sexual harassment. Most often, however, there are several types of sexually harassing behaviors present, and, there is no minimum level for harassing conduct under the law. The general rule is that the more severe the conduct, the less number of times it has to occur. Ultimately, each case turns on its own facts—how severe the conduct was and how the conduct impacted the target of the harassment.

"CONTINUUM" OF HARM

There are different degrees of sexual harassment. The less physically threatening forms of sexually harassing behaviors are also the most commonly reported. These include:

- sexual jokes;
- sexual comments;
- sexual questions;
- sexual teasing;
- inappropriate sexual advances; and,
- requests for sex.

Less common, but more violent, sexually harassing conduct includes:

- threats;
- forced sexual touching; or,
- attempted sexual assault.

Sexist Words

Sometimes sexual harassment takes the form of words that are directed at females in general, such as:

- calling a woman "doll," "babe," or "honey;"
- using sexist phrases, like "dumb blondes;"
- asserting that "women cry more;"
- asking male workers to "think above the belt buckles this morning;"
- announcing that "women can't manage" or "workers won't work for a woman;"
- claiming that "some jobs are just women's work;" or,
- suggesting that women should be "barefoot and pregnant."

CASE

It was sexual harassment for a male supervisor to tell a female employee that women are "too emotional" to be in the workplace, that they need sex in order to perform well, and that violence may be the only way to keep a woman in line. (Smith v. First Union Nat'l Bank, 202 F.3d 234 (4th Cir. 2000).)

Sexist Behavior

A harasser's physical conduct may also contribute to a sexually harassing environment. Examples of sexually harassing conduct without words include:

- looking a person up and down (elevator eyes);
- staring at someone;
- cornering a person or blocking a person's path;
- following the person;
- giving personal gifts;
- hanging around a person;
- intentionally standing too close to or brushing against a person;
- looking up a skirt or down a blouse;
- pulling a person onto one's lap;
- displaying sexist or sexual calendars;
- writing sexist or sexual graffiti;
- massaging or touching a person's clothing, hair or body;
- hugging, kissing, patting or stroking;
- touching or rubbing oneself sexually around another person;
- making facial expressions such as winking, throwing kisses or licking lips;
- making sexual gestures with hands or through body movements; or,
- making "catcalls" or whistling suggestively or engaging in lip smacking.

A high school student complained that her teacher, on a daily basis, stared at her breasts and body parts and went out of his way to spend a lot of time with her, frequently standing over her with his hand on her chair at school. He also placed his hand on her buttocks and inner thigh, put his arms around her and touched her breast, and pushed his pelvis against her buttocks. During these

CASE

(continued)

> times, he made numerous comments, such as telling her to tell her boyfriend that he was "lucky" and that "It's hard to think of you as a student." Her teacher also repeatedly invited her to his house, stating that he wanted to photograph her and show her his photographs. (*Morlock v. West Cent. Educ. Dist.*, 46 F. Supp. 2d 892 (D.Minn. 1999).)

Sexual Advances

Some harassment may include physical and verbal sexual advances towards one or more victims. Examples of these are:

- turning discussions to sexual topics;
- telling sexually explicit or suggestive jokes or stories;
- asking about sexual fantasies, experiences, preferences or history;
- making sexual comments or innuendos;
- telling lies or spreading rumors about a person's sex life;
- asking personal questions about social or sexual life;
- making sexual comments about a person's clothing, anatomy or looks;
- repeatedly asking out a person who is not interested; or,
- making harassing phone calls or e-mails.

Requests for Sex

This type of sexually harassing behavior typically occurs where a supervisor or teacher suggests or promises benefits, like a promotion, wage increase, or better grade if the victim engages in sexual activity. These requests include:

- asking a person to "spend the night" or have an affair; or
- asking a person to have sex or "make out."

A young New Jersey woman left her job after six weeks because the president of her company, among other things, constantly asked her to have sex with him and on several occasions grabbed her and tried to kiss her. (*Schmidt v. Smith*, 684 A.2d 66 (N.J.Super.1996).)

CASE

Sexual Intimidation

This type of coercion occurs when there is a warning that the employee will lose her job, lose a job benefit, or perhaps get a failing grade unless the employee or student agrees to engage in a sexual activity. For example:

- •telling a person to go to a motel to "negotiate" a raise; or
- •ordering a person to provide sexual services to avoid a transfer.

A male oil rig worker complained that he was forcibly subjected to sex-related, humiliating actions by certain co-workers and he quit to avoid being raped or forced to have sex with these men. (*Oncale v. Sundowner Offshore Services, Inc.*, 118 S.Ct. 1002 (1998).)

CASE

Sexual Criminal Conduct

Physically grabbing, touching or forcing sexual activity is a sexual crime. These include committing:

- •forced sexual touching;
- •sexual assault or rape; or,
- •sexual battery.

A disabled student who functioned at the level of a first-grader was battered and sexually assaulted by another student who had started by making sexually aggressive advances toward her. This progressed to threatening phone

(continued)

CASE

calls and, finally, to taking the victim to a secluded part of the school and sexually assaulting her. As a result, she had to undergo medical and psychiatric treatment after she began to engage in self-destructive and suicidal behavior. (*Murrell v. School Dist. No. 1*, 186 F.3d 1238 (10th Cir. 1999).)

TYPES OF SEXUAL HARASSMENT

2

Courts have identified two general types of sexual harassment that extend to other more specific forms. One general type is called *quid pro quo*, which means "something for something." The other general type is called "hostile environment." In both cases, the law requires that the conduct was *unwelcome*. This means that the person did not invite it. Many employers have policies about relationships between employees. In a school setting, if the harasser is in a position of authority, (like a teacher), the issue of whether the conduct is *welcome* will only arise with adult students. There are also some things *not* considered sexually harassing, and those will be discussed on page 14.

QUID PRO QUO

A *quid pro quo* type case usually involves a supervisor or teacher who has the power to make decisions about the employee or student based on whether he or she submits to sexual demands.

> A young woman worked for an equipment rental company as a forklift manager. For two years, the president of the company, repeatedly asked her and other women workers to reach into the front pocket of his pants to retrieve coins. He
>
> *(continued)*

CASE

> also threw items to the ground in front of them and asked them to bend over in front of him and pick the items up. He frequently made sexual comments when referring to the women's clothing. He also told the young forklift manager: "you're a woman, what do you know," "you're a dumb ass woman," and "we need a man as the rental manager." He also told her in front of other employees and a client, that they should go to a motel to negotiate her raise.
> (*Harris v. Forklift Sys., Inc.*, 510 U.S. 17 (1993).)

CASE

> A high school teacher engaged in a pattern of directing inappropriate suggestive remarks towards a female eighth grade student when he led a book discussion group. He also visited her at her home when he knew she would be alone. Beginning when she was a freshman in his class, he had sex with her many times; often while classes were in session.
> (*Gebser v. Lago Vista Independent School District*, 524 U.S. 274 (1998).)

In the above cases, when the president of the company told the woman that they needed to go to a motel to "negotiate" her raise, it was *quid pro quo* sexual harassment. The law does not require the employee to submit to the demand. This is because the sexual advance or demand became an illegal condition of the job. Similarly, the teacher who abused his power to have sex with the 9th grader engaged in *quid pro quo* sexual harassment because the sex became a condition of the class.

What Happens When There Was a Former Relationship?

Voluntary and welcomed sexual conduct between co-workers or students is not prohibited by law. In fact, many people meet their future spouses or significant others as fellow classmates at school or as co-workers. Because the conduct once was welcomed, the person who has ended the relationship must make it clear to the other person that further sexual advances are no longer welcome. This can be done in person, but sending a letter or other written document stating that further advances are not welcome may be helpful to show a present intent that the conduct is not—and will not be—welcome.

> A supervisor convinced his female employee to have sex with him. After she broke it off, he agreed to treat her in a professional manner, but when his employee asked about a promotion, the supervisor told her he was still sexually attracted to her and suggested that they have sex. She declined and he promoted her, but later told her that she "owed" him for her promotion.
> (*Henningsen v. Worldcom*, 9 P.3d 948 (Wash.App. 2000).)

CASE

HOSTILE ENVIRONMENT

A *hostile environment* case is established when the environment becomes so intimidating or offensive that it changes the conditions of the job or denies an educational opportunity to a student. A hostile environment can be caused by the sexual harassment of teachers, students or third parties.

> A woman welder was constantly subjected to pornographic pictures posted on the walls of her workplace. Male co-workers referred to her as "baby," "sugar," "momma," and "dear." Obscene drawings and graffiti referring to the woman were placed throughout the workplace. Pornographic pictures were often put into her work materials. (*Robinson v. Jacksonville Shipyards, Inc.*, 760 F. Supp. 1486 (M.D. Fla. 1991).)

CASE

CASE

Over a period of five months, a fifth grade girl was repeatedly sexually harassed by a classmate who sat next to her at school. On several occasions, he attempted to touch her breasts and genitals; gestured at her while rubbing his body in a sexually suggestive manner; and, made sexually explicit statements to her. (*Davis v. Monroe County Board of Education*, 526 U.S. 629, 119 S. Ct. 1661 (1999).)

All of the circumstances of the environment are examined, including:

- the conduct itself (nature, type, how often, for how long and where the conduct occurred);
- the persons involved (age and sex of the parties, the number of accused);
- whether an accused harasser was in a position of power;
- whether the conduct negatively affected the work or school environment; and,
- whether any other incidents of sexual harassment occurred in the workplace or school.

Whether an environment is hostile is determined by examining how many times the conduct occurred, the severity of the conduct, and the effect it had on the victim.

NOTE: *The law recognizes that others are discriminated against when sexual harassment is present in the workplace or at school. Consequently, a victim of sexual harassment does not have to be the person harassed, but could be anyone affected by the offensive conduct.*

ONE INCIDENT CONSTITUTING SEXUAL HARASSMENT

The general rule is that the more severe the harassment, the less need to show more than one incident. For example, in a *quid pro quo* case, a single sexual advance may be enough to show sexual harassment where it is connected to granting or denying school or employment benefits.

However, unless the conduct is very serious, a single incident of offensive sexual conduct or comment generally does not create a *hostile environment*. This type of claim usually requires a showing of a pattern offensive conduct. A single, unusually severe incident of harassment may be sufficient, however. (For example, a single touching of a classmate's or co-workers' intimate body areas is considered sexual harassment.)

SEXUAL JOKING

Sexual harassment exists only where the conduct is "unwelcome," unless the target is a minor. Therefore, while some women think that if they join in the joking it will lessen the impact of the harassment, in fact it may work against her. It provides evidence that she did not find it objectionable or offensive and may result in a determination that she was not a victim of a hostile environment. In fact, going along with the jokes is not effective in stopping harassment and, in a significant number of cases, just makes it worse.

As unfair as it may seem, the law permits review of "provocative dress" and "bad language" and other conduct of the target of harassment. There are several cases in which complaints of sexual harassment were denied because the target "participated in sexual horseplay" or used vulgar or foul language herself. Ultimately though, the determination of whether a work environment is hostile is made after reviewing all of the circumstances and the context in which the behavior occurred.

THOSE THINGS CONSIDERED NOT TO BE SEXUALLY HARASSING CONDUCT

While there are few bright lines in the area of sexual harassment, most cases can be determined by looking at the circumstances surrounding the conduct. Is it physical? Is it severe? Is it intended to be hurtful or disrespectful? How does the person respond to the behavior or conduct? However, in an effort to err on the side of being careful, it is true that some silly decisions about what is sexual harassment have been made in recent years. Take the following cases, for example:

> **CASE**
>
> A North Carolina, six-year-old was punished for sexually harassing a classmate by kissing her on the cheek. (See "Kiss and Tell; Alas, What Fools These School Officials Be," COLUMBUS DISPATCH, Sept.28, 1996, 8A.)

> **CASE**
>
> A seven-year-old was suspended for sexually harassing a classmate by kissing her because he liked her, and yanking at her skirt button because in his favorite book, *Corduroy*, a teddy bear was missing a button. (See "2nd School Suspension for a Stolen Kiss is Cut Short," L.A. TIMES, Oct. 3, 1996, at A14.)

The Supreme Court has recently made clear that unless the conduct is physically invasive (like grabbing a breast), a victim must usually show a *pattern* of harassing behavior in order to demonstrate a legal claim for sexual harassment. This is because the anti-discrimination laws are not a "general civility code." Teasing, general comments, or isolated instances of sexual conduct will not usually rise to the level of a legal case of sexual harassment. Also, flirting or isolated joking is not usually considered sufficient to show sexual harassment.

It was not sexual harassment but just "the ordinary tribulations of the workplace" where, over a period of six to seven months, a supervisor asked the plaintiff to lunch several times, told her she looked "very beautiful" and put his hand on her knee one time. (<u>Gupta v. Florida Board of Regents</u>, 212 F.3d 571 (11th Cir. 2000).)

CASE

WHY SEXUAL HARASSMENT OCCURS

3

Sexual harassment is more about power than about sex, and it is the abuse of power that is the key to understanding why sexual harassment occurs.

THE REASONS WHY STUDENTS HARASS

Students in particular have a unique position on harassment. In one comprehensive study of more than 1600 students, those who admitted that they had harassed other students explained that, "it's just a part of school life. A lot of people do it. It's no big deal." (See AAUW, Hostile Hallways study.) Researchers believe that the true reasons—to assert power and induce fear in their victims—lay the foundation for sexual harassment. This develops and continues throughout high school, the hazing behaviors of college, and finally appears in the workplace.

SEXUAL STEREOTYPING

Sexual harassment can occur in any workplace. In fact, in the very first survey of 9000 women, there was little difference in the type of workplace identified by women who said they were sexually harassed. But, the results of numerous studies show that one of the factors that is present in a high percentage of sexual harassment cases is a workplace that encourages "traditional" attitudes towards women.

These workplaces have attitudes, such as:

- she does not belong in this job;
- she does not belong in the workplace;
- she is taking the place of a man who needs the job;
- she is being paid more than a woman ought to earn; and,
- she is just at this job to find a husband.

These views stereotype women by their sex rather than as workers.

Male-dominated workplaces

High levels of sexual harassment exist when there is a low number of women in the workplace. The more nontraditional the job for women, the more likely the sexual harassment. Female doctors and investment bankers rank among the highest for harassment. (See "Sexual Harassment: It's About Power, Not Lust." *New York Times*. (1991)(Oct.22,1991).)

When women do break into these fields and do achieve success, those men who believe the stereotype that males are superior, feel threatened by the entry of females. Sexual harassment is one way to "put down" the female to "keep her in her place" and to increase the feeling of power by the harasser. If the woman becomes frustrated enough, she may begin to make mistakes, "get sick," be absent from work or fail to carry out the job, leaving the harasser with the satisfaction of knowing that "women just cannot make it in a man's world."

Where few women workers are present in a workplace, they are singled out for scrutiny and are the focus of attention for the rumormill. When these workers make a mistake on the job, it typically causes extreme responses from the males who comprise the majority group. Mistakes that would be minor if a male worker committed them become perceived as much worse when the few women commit them.

For example, in a 1981 survey of women coal miners, 17% reported having been physically attacked on the job, 53% reported propositions from their supervisors on at least one occasion, and 76% reported propositions from a co-worker. ("Sexual Harassment in the Coal Industry: A Survey of Women Miners. Oak Ridge, Tennessee: Coal Employment Project." as reported in *New York Times* (Oct. 22, 1991).) A study of college graduates employed in male-populated occupations of engineering and management also reported a high percentage of sexual harassment. (See Lafontaine, E. and L. Treadeau. "The Frequency, Sources, and Correlates of Sexual Harassment among Women in Traditional Male Occupations." Sex Roles, pp.433-442 (1986)(160 women surveyed).) The similarity was that these women were in traditionally male jobs.

In policing, for example, in 2001, women comprised only 12.7% of all police officers nationwide — only 4% more than in 1990, when women made up 9% of officers. (National Center for Women & Policing, *Equality Denied: THE STATUS OF WOMEN IN POLICING: 2001* (April, 2002).) Women held about 7% of sworn top command law enforcement positions in large agencies, but only 4% in smaller or rural agencies, and just 9% of supervisory positions in these departments. More than 56% of the agencies surveyed reported no women in top command positions. Numerous cases of sexual harassment are reported every year in police agencies throughout the country:

In 1995, the Los Angeles Police Department settled a sexual harassment case involving a 1990 rape of a female officer who was sexually assaulted by a fellow male officer who followed her into a women's bathroom at the Police Academy lounge when she was ill from intoxication. At the time of the settlement, there were over two dozen sexual harassment

(continued)

CASE

cases pending filed by female officers in the department. Prior to settling the case, the victim testified to repeated incidents of harassment by male officers while she was on duty, starting when she joined the department in 1987 until she left patrol in 1992. (See LAPD Settles ACLU Sexual Assault Case for $165,000; Case Symbolizes Persistent Sexual Harassment, Gender Inequities (January 25, 1995).)

CASE

In Grand Rapids, Michigan, nine female police officers sued the city and its police department, naming more than 20 male officers and implicating several command-level officers in allegations of sexual harassment occurring between 1996 and 2000. Allegations included:
- unwanted physical advances;
- crude and demeaning insults;
- being assigned to do "women's work," such as filing;
- death threats from male officers while on the job;
- a male sergeant pointed a loaded gun at one of the female officers and warned her to keep quiet about on-duty sexual advances; and,
- exclusions from promotions and assignments.

Besides the nine women who filed the lawsuit, nearly 30 current and past female officers and trainees are listed in the suit as possible victims. Of the city's nearly 400 police officers, about 50 are women.

(Grand Rapids, Michigan. AP: January 26, 2001.)

SEXUAL HARASSMENT IS COMMON IN THE MILITARY

Just about half the women in the Air Force, Army and Navy reported sexual harassment. In 1996, in the national surveys of federal workers conducted by the Merit Systems Protection Board, cases of rape in the Army surfaced and when the Army established a sexual harassment hotline, it received nearly 6,600 complaints in its first two months.

In one particularly outrageous example, a female helicopter pilot was one of more than 80 women who said they were sexually assaulted by drunken Navy and Marine pilots at the 1991 Tailhook convention.(See also "Two Out of Three Women in Military Study Report Sexual Harassment Incidents," page A22. *The New York Times.* P.A22 (Sept. 12, 1991).) When she stepped out of an elevator in her hotel, she was forced to run a gauntlet of officers who grabbed at her breasts, her crotch and buttocks, and attempted to tear her clothes from her body. When her complaints to her Admiral boss went nowhere, she filed a formal complaint with the Navy before resigning her commission. She eventually filed a civil lawsuit and won $5 million in damages.

The Navy went on to determine that 117 officers were "implicated in one or more incidents of indecent assault, indecent exposure, conduct unbecoming an officer, or failure to act in a proper leadership capacity." Eventually, over seventy officers, including admirals, captains and commanders of the Navy and Marines were disciplined. Because of this case, there were changes of policy within the U.S. military. Still, as of 1999, there were just 300 women among the 10,000 pilots in the Navy and Marines.

Cases of sexual harassment in the military continue to be reported, like the December 1999 cases of an Army drill sergeant who was court-martialed for fondling or sexually harassing twenty female recruits in his command.

CASE

The drill sergeant at Fort Jackson, South Carolina sexually harassed and assaulted female trainees from July 1995 until April 1996, when he was reported by a recruit who said he followed her into the female sleeping bay and rubbed his hand

(continued)

across her hair and breast. He then engaged in an effort to dissuade her from cooperating in the investigation and tried to get another female recruit to wrongfully offer a statement against her. (See *U.S. v. Barner*, 00-0431 (U.S. Ct of App, Armed Forces 2001).)

SEXIST WORKPLACE

The type of workplace also is a factor in stereotyping. A workplace which is full of sexist pictures or joking or sexual slurs may contribute to the view of women as stereotypical sex objects. There is a connection between the presence of pictures and sexual comments and the level of sexual preoccupation of some male workers whose conduct has sexual overtones towards female workers.

CASES

As one court has noted:

[T]he effect of pornography on workplace equality is obvious. Pornography on an employer's wall or desk communicates a message about the way he views women, a view strikingly at odds with the way women wish to be viewed in the workplace. Depending upon the material in question, it may communicate that women should be the objects of sexual aggression, that they are submissive slaves to male desires, or that their most salient and desirable attributes are sexual. Any of these images may communicate to male co-workers that it is acceptable to view women in a predominately sexual way. All of the views to some extent detract from the image most women in the workplace would like to project: that of the professional, credible co-worker.(*EEOC v. Dial Corp.*, 156 F. Supp. 2d 926 (N.D. Ill.2001)(discussing *Robinson v. Jacksonville Shipyards, Inc.*, 760 F. Supp. 1486 (M.D. Fla. 1991).)

Male Supervisors

The type of power structure in a workplace also affects sex stereotyping. Often in this type of workplace, the workers affected by the sexualized working conditions are women and the people deciding what to do about it are men. So men, who are typically the supervisors in this type of workplace, and who are the ones to get complaints from women, tend to ignore or minimize the complaints.

SEXUALIZED ENVIRONMENT

Another factor which contributes to sex stereotyping is the climate of the workplace. For example, when obscenities are common in the workplace, women are three times more likely to be treated as sex objects than in a workplace where profanity is not tolerated. And, when sexual joking is common in a work environment, stereotyping of women as sex objects is three to seven times more likely to occur.

Sexual stereotyping has serious consequences for women. One expert explained that: "when sex comes into the workplace, women are profoundly affected in their job performance and in their ability to do their jobs without being bothered by it." This is because men and women perceive the existence of sexual harassment differently. Fear of harassment for women may also involve the very real, potential risk of harm if obnoxious words or "jokes" turn into threats or sexual violence. Therefore, women and the studies show that girls in school who are sexually harassed are more likely to be negatively affected by it than are males.

In workplaces which are controlled by men and in which few women work in a given location, if a woman complains about a man who exposed himself to her, it is the woman that will be perceived as the problem. She may become the subject of rumors. The male worker will not likely be disciplined or if disciplined, it will be slight. In one court case, this took the form of the supervisor who said that the woman's complaint that her co-worker exposed himself to her was "one person's word against another's." The same thing may happen in a workplace which has sexualized pictures of women displayed. She may be seen in such a workplace as a "complainer" and a "problem" employee. Other workers may speculate on her sexuality or try to find out "what is wrong with her."

Women who work in this type of workplace may begin to monitor their own behavior to try to avoid sexual attention from males in the workplace. Or they may try to join in the stereotyping, becoming overly "sexy" or "flirty," telling dirty jokes themselves so that they can "fit in" and avoid being ostracized. Some women may become rigid, refusing to engage in the workplace "banter" and so become the focus of intensified harassment as the next case shows.

CASE

A woman plant worker reported that male co-workers made various sexual comments about her body. Nothing was done about her complaint and the co-worker continued his pattern of harassment, soon joined by another. The two were boldly making comments to others and reporting on graffiti now appearing on the men's bathroom walls. She continued to report to no avail. Her own supervisor grabbed her breast and asked her out for drinks at a local bar. She declined, and complained to a higher up who said he would talk to the supervisor and not to take him too seriously. Male co-workers developed sexualized nicknames for her and her supervisor gave her a performance review form containing sexual content. Other supervisors joined in the sexualized commentary directed at this worker. Untrue rumors were constantly

(continued)

circulated about her sexual activities. Other co-workers began to target her for sexual conversations and gestures. She continued to complain and was terminated in a "work-force reduction" even though three days before she was fired the company approved a budget which forecasted an increase. No other employee was terminated as a result of the "downsizing."

(*Baty v. Williamette Ind., Inc.*, 172 F.3d 1232 (10th Cir.1999).)

SEXUAL HARASSMENT AND PREJUDICE

Sexual harassment may also occur out of a bias or prejudice. It is common for people to associate with others who are like themselves. Some call this the "like me syndrome." Supervisors may have it and want to hire or promote persons who look and act like themselves. For example, this type of supervisor may think "women are too weak to be in management." Also, work relationships and friendships are often formed with persons who look and act like us. The "like me" prejudice may also be found in a work evaluations. Someone who is perceived of as "different" may get tougher appraisals of their performance.

THE IMPACT OF SEXUAL HARASSMENT

4

"My stomach would get sick . . . . I had nightmares . . .it made my [male and female] co-workers uncomfortable . . . so it affected all of us." *comment from respondent 1994 Merit Systems Protection Board (MSPB) survey.*

Sexual harassment can cause serious harm to its victims, their families and other classmates or co-workers. Sexual harassment also has a destructive effect on an entire workplace or school. The sexual harassment victim's work performance declines as the stress of sexual harassment distracts the victim from her work. Her co-worker friends or fellow students become less productive as they spend work time strategizing on ways to solve the problem. Employers are especially impacted because every year hundreds of millions of dollars are lost in disrupted productivity. Ultimately there is a turnover of tens of thousands of experienced women employees and students.

> Where a sixth grader was repeatedly sexually harassed by a student teacher and other boys and the school principal failed to remedy the situation, the child left school never to return. (See Oona v. McCaffrey, 143 F.3d 473 (9th Cir. 1998).)
>
> CASE

Emotional effects

Emotional trauma can be as disabling to a person as a visible physical wound. Sexual harassment is humiliating and degrading and can cause victims to suffer a loss of self-confidence and self-esteem. They often feel embarrassed, and ashamed at being targeted for abuse. Most report being scared, nervous, irritable, and suffering crying spells. They may feel that they don't know how to stop it or when it will end. At times, they feel tremendous anger over their situation. As the effects of the sexual harassment are compounded over time, victims may have difficulty concentrating and feel helpless and isolated and vulnerable. Ultimately, they may become depressed, have anxiety attacks and even a nervous breakdown.

CASE

Where a young woman was sexually harassed for a period of six weeks, she suffered severe emotional distress. She relapsed into an earlier eating disorder and substance abuse, and attempted suicide as a result of the sexual harassment.
(*Schmidt v. Smith*, 684 A.2d 66 (N.J.Super.1996).)

Physical effects

Emotional distress can, and often does, have a direct effect on other bodily functions. Physically the symptoms of stress can be seen in women whose weight fluctuates. Their stomach may be upset and they may begin vomiting or stop eating, causing weight loss. Or, they may seek comfort in food and gain considerable weight. Victims also report having heart palpitations or high blood pressure. Many are fatigued, feeling tired all the time. Often, victims report headaches and muscle aches. Their worry and anxiety may make it hard for them to sleep or give them nightmares. They may also have hives or experience allergic reactions. Alcohol and substance abuse have also been reported as victims attempt to numb the stress of the workplace.

THE SPECIFIC IMPACT ON STUDENTS

Sexual harassment exacts a terrible price on its youngest victims. Stereotypes that harassment is just "teasing" and that kids "will grow out of it" fail to recognize that the harm caused by sexual harassment can be very severe indeed.

For months, an 11-year-old girl was targeted by a boy in her class. He threatened her, made obscene gestures and called her names. Her father reported that the school's unwillingness to stop the sexual harassment meant that his daughter suffered. He said she was "sullen and isolated...She would come home and lock the door to her room" as her "self-esteem withered away." (See Tamar Lewin, "Kissing Cases Highlight Schools' Fears of Liability for Sexual Harassment." N.Y. Times, A22 (Oct. 6, 1996).)

CASE

Victims may not wish to stay in, or return to, school. They may not want to participate in class activities. They often have difficulty paying attention to lessons and so their studies suffer. They may begin to drop in grades and may ultimately drop out altogether. For example in a study called Hostile Hallways, about one-third of the girls who were sexually harassed in grade school and early high school years reported wanting to quit school and receiving a lower class grade.

Depending on their emotional maturity, sexual harassment interferes with the healthy development of their views of how male-female relationships are or should be.

CASE

Two 11 year-old boys terrorized a ten year old girl by knocking her to the ground twenty to thirty times while at school and sexually fondled her while threatening to sexually assault her. One time the victim passed a note to the teacher asking for help, but the teacher tore it up, calling her a "tattletale." When the school principal was notified, she called the boys in and when they admitted their conduct, gave them a one-day, in-school suspension. The boys did not stop, however, and the sexual harassment caused the victim to miss many days of school, resulting in lowered grades and an inability to complete required course work. The girl's mental health also suffered and she had to be seen by a psychiatrist.
(See *Metropolitan Gov't of Davidson County*, 32 F. Supp. 2d 991, 996 (M.D. Tenn. 1998).)

Girls perceive sexual harassment as much more serious than boys do. For example, in one study, nearly 76% of boys said that they would feel good if a girl shouted to a boy that he had a "hot outfit," but only 12% of girls did. Girls also report being much more upset and feeling fearful and helpless over the sexual harassment than did boys. In the Hostile Hallways study, for example, 50% of the students who experienced sexual harassment were embarrassed. Most suffered a loss of self esteem. In one study of young students, more than 57% of the girls, but only 17% of the boys reported feeling "scared" by sexual harassment. Girls, also, try to avoid the situations in which sexual harassment occurs. For example, they might avoid the harasser by giving up attendance at school functions. (See "The Experience of Sexual Harassment Among Grad-School Students: Early Socialization of Female Subordination?" *Sex Roles: A Journal of Research* (July 2000).)

> **CASE**
>
> A developmentally disabled victim of repeated sexual harassment and sexual assault engaged in self-destructive and suicidal behavior and was ultimately hospitalized for psychiatric care.
> (*Murrell v. School Dist. No. 1*, 186 F.3d 1238 (10th cir. 1999).)

Older students also suffer from some of the same effects. They may have difficulty concentrating on classwork, feel isolated and at risk, fear for their safety and drop a class or out of school completely as a result of the sexual harassment. (See Hostile Hallways.)

Students often feel embarrassed and self-conscious. They may lose confidence and feel a pervading sense of fear. They may develop serious depression as a result. Without the support and intervention of school authorities, they may simply be unable to overcome the devastating impact of the severe harassment.

> **CASE**
>
> In 1985 in Minnesota, 15 year old Kathi was assaulted at a hockey tournament by three teen-age hockey players who she knew from her high school. She pressed charges and they were found guilty of sexual assault. But back at school, Kathi faced the loss of her friends; she was called sexually derogatory names and death threats were written on her locker, because "she took our friends to court." The offenders were treated as school heroes; they only missed one hockey game. Kathi tried to stay in school, but a few days after her 18th birthday, she couldn't take it anymore. She committed suicide. (See Doug Grow, "Suicide Ended Kathi's 'Fight for Dignity,'" *Star Tribune* p.1 (July 5, 1987).)

THE SPECIFIC IMPACT ON THE WORKER

Sexual harassment also causes harm to its victims that goes far beyond the workplace. Victims suffer physical, mental, emotional and financial loss that can be devastating. The National Institute for Occupational Safety and Health (NIOSH) has reported recently that working women face higher risks than men from job-related stress, and one of the most "noxious" stressors is sexual harassment.

Most victims experience stress-related conditions that can be traumatic. In one study, 96% of sexual harassment victims experienced emotional stress, about half suffered work performance stress, and over a third had physical stress problems. In fact, sexual harassment causes so many damaging physical, mental and emotional effects on its victims that the American Psychiatric Association has recognized that it is a severe stressor that can contribute to a serious mental health condition called post-traumatic stress disorder. Sexual harassment also affects the victim's relationships with their families. Friendships both inside and out of the workplace are affected.

Economic effects

Sexual harassment may have severe economic effects on a victim. A woman may be denied educational opportunities or a promotion or raise. She may be reassigned to a difficult position or transferred away from her family and support. Many women leave their jobs every year and face unemployment. The effects of sexual harassment may follow her from the workplace, because it may have an effect on her work record and references.

Recognizing the terrible impact of sexual harassment on victims can help you to protect yourself from its debilitating effects, and decide on a strategy that will end the harassment. (See Chapter 5.)

WHAT YOU CAN DO ABOUT SEXUAL HARASSMENT

5

How a person handles any crisis depends on his or her personality and the circumstances that are faced. Most harassers will continue as long as they can, and unless they quit or get transferred, the harassment is unlikely to stop. But there are several strategies which can help to end this obnoxious abuse of power. Choosing the strategy that is best for you depends on the severity of the harassment and on your own circumstances.

Whether you are sexually harassed at work or school, your choices are pretty straightforward. You can ignore it or do nothing. You can make a joke of it. You can avoid the harasser if possible. You can ask or tell the harasser to stop. You can threaten to tell someone or report the harasser.

On the following page, compare two surveys of thousands of workers, the first taken in the 80s and the second in the 90s. In the first survey, it was determined that over 36,000 workers left their jobs due to sexual harassment, by the second, nearly 20,000 workers did.

HOW WORKERS RESPOND WHEN FACED WITH SEXUAL HARASSMENT

ACTION	1987 workers	1994 workers
Ignored it or did nothing	52%	44%
Avoided the harasser	43%	28%
Asked/told the harasser to stop	44%	35%
Made a joke of it	20%	15%
Threatened to tell someone	14%	10%
Reported the harasser	15%	12%
Submitted to the harassment	4%	7%

Note: Employees surveyed could make more than one choice

Source: U.S. Merit Systems Protection Board, Sexual Harassment of Federal Workers: An Update. Washington, D.C.: U.S.Gov't Printing Office (1987); and. U.S. Merit Systems Protection Board, Sexual Harassment in the Federal Workplace: Trends, Progress, Continuing Challenges. Washington, D.C.: U.S. Gov't Printing Office (1994).

The above chart shows that when faced with sexual harassment, most women:
- ignored it;
- denied it; or,
- avoided the harasser or the environment.

Some were able to confront the harasser. Others joined in the joking or sexual banter in order to feel like they have some control over the situation. Finally, and rarely, victims threatened to report or filed a grievance or complaint.

STRATEGIES TO STOP SEXUAL HARASSMENT

So what is the best strategy to stop sexual harassment? Does the fact that most women ignored the harassment or avoided the harasser mean that these are best? Should you confront him? While every woman must decide for herself what will work, it is important to consider the outcome of the choices made by the women who have already faced harassment.

Ignore It

The most common response to sexual harassment is to ignore the conduct. This allows the victim to keep on working in the hope that it will "just go away." Unfortunately, ignoring the harassment may be read by the harasser as a license to continue. After all, in the harasser's mind, the harassment has not had the desired effect unless the victim is affected by it. The harasser may become bolder or intensify his efforts. Ignoring sexual harassment will rarely stop it.

Deny It

Many women simply deny that what is happening is sexual harassment. The notion that "this can't be happening" or "he was just kidding" helps to retain the notion that you have control over your work environment. Some challenge their own feelings by minimizing what is happening and that "it wasn't that serious." Others discount their experience thinking, "I'm imagining things" or "I'm overreacting." While denial is a protective strategy, the harasser has time to continue and often escalate his behavior.

Avoid It

When denial becomes impossible, the victim may question whether she is somehow at fault. She may change her appearance or dress in an effort to end the harassment. She may avoid being near the harasser whenever possible. None of these things will end the harassment, because the victim is not the cause of the harassment.

It is common for victims to take sick or vacation leave. Sometimes she may request a transfer or reassignment or even quit to end the harassment. While leaving the workplace will remove the victim from the harassment, loss of sick or vacation leave and certainly loss of a job are a high price to pay to end the harassment. And, sometimes, especially if there has been a past relationship, the harasser knows where the victim lives and continues his conduct outside of the workplace.

Joining in the Sexual "Bantering"

Some victims do join in the workplace bantering, using vulgar language and acting in a sexualized manner. This is one way to live the illusion that, by becoming "one of the guys," one will not get further harassed. But while victims perceive the joining as a way of controlling or defusing the harassment, courts see it as contributing to the sexual conduct in the workplace and may decide that the behavior was "welcomed" because of the victim's response. Also, women who have gone along with the harassment report it was the least effective thing they could have done. In fact, in many cases, the harassment gets worse.

Confront the Harasser

Only about one-third of women who are sexually harassed ask or tell the harasser to stop his conduct. Yet, this is the most effective strategy to ending the harassment. Try to gain the support of your friends in the workplace to also put pressure on the harasser to stop his conduct. Ask your employer to set up a training surrounding sexual harassment.

If you are not at risk of harm, say something like:
- "your conduct is not acceptable;"
- "you are not funny;"
- "your conduct /behavior is hurtful;"
- "it is not a joke;"
- "it is degrading;" or,
- "stop it!"

Say it firmly and with conviction. It is important to note that it can be helpful under the law that you let the harasser know that his conduct is "unwelcome."

It may be that the harasser is a beginner or just a clod and totally insensitive. It is possible that the harasser does not realize the behavior is offensive. Your clear words will put the harasser on notice that his comments, jokes, conduct or innuendo are simply not appropriate. Sometimes, if it is less severe form of harassment, or a beginning harasser, a clear direct statement from you (and from your co-workers) to stop may be all that is needed to end the behavior.

If it is too stressful to talk to the person who is harassing you, write a letter. In the letter, clearly state the behavior that is offensive to you. For example, say "several times you have stared at me and followed me around the office. You have put your hands on my shoulders to give me a 'massage.' You even suggested that I could 'get ahead' in the company if I went to a motel with you." Include dates and locations of this conduct. Tell the harasser to stop. Tell him that the conduct makes you feel uncomfortable or threatened. Keep the letter on a professional level. Make sure to keep a copy of the letter for later use at a more formal proceeding if necessary.

Report the Harassment

Historically, few victims report the harassment to their employer. Very few—maybe as low as 5-10%—choose to file a complaint with an outside agency. Why don't victims report? They believe that others won't take it seriously. Some fear what would happen to them at work if they reported. They are embarrassed at the notion of reporting and fear retaliation at the workplace. Some believe that nothing could be done. Others don't think that they would be believed or think they would be blamed. Some women do not report because they do not wish to hurt the person who is harassing them. Yet, when women do report sexual harassment, the majority of the time, the situation improves.

Most employers have policies addressing sexual harassment and may allow informal and formal complaints. You may also choose to file a complaint with the EEOC or your state fair employment practice agency. These options are detailed in later sections of the book.

WHATEVER ELSE YOU DO— DOCUMENT THE HARASSMENT

Although the experience of victims who have been through sexual harassment shows that confronting the harasser or reporting the harassment is the most effective way to stop it, while you are deciding on your best strategy, be sure to keep a record of every instance of harassment.

Take good notes of every incident of harassment and keep them in a protected place away from your workplace. Use a notebook or diary. Make sure you document all the following information:

- Who was present? Always list who was there. Besides you and the harasser, who heard or saw the harassment? Put down complete names whenever possible.
- What happened? Use quotes to record the comments, words, or jokes. Describe exactly what the conduct was. Include any contextual information, such as what happened just before or after that related to the conduct or words.
- When did it happen? The time and date should be included.
- Where did it happen? Make sure you record the exact room or location. If harassment happens outside the workplace, document that also.

Make sure you also document how each incident affected you. Also, be sure to gather any evidence of harassment. Is there a picture, photo, diagram, or drawing of the harassment. Is it in a note or letter? Is it an e-mail? If possible, get the exact item or photo or print a copy to keep with your documents for future use, if necessary.

SECTION TWO:

Sexual Harassment in the Workplace

SEXUAL HARASSMENT IN EMPLOYMENT: THE LAW

6

Laws that prohibit sexual harassment exist on the federal, state, and local level. The federal anti-discrimination law that prohibits sexual harassment in the workplace is Title VII of the Civil Rights Act of 1964. Most states have also passed Fair Employment Practice Acts which are modeled after federal laws. All states and some municipalities have passed anti-discrimination laws and provide another option to pursue a claim of employment discrimination. The conduct underlying sexual harassment may also form the basis of private lawsuits. In some cases, it may also be prohibited by criminal laws.

TITLE VII OF THE CIVIL RIGHTS ACT

The relevant part of Title VII of the Civil Rights Act can be found in Appendix C. If you read the law, you will realize that the words "sexual harassment" do not appear in the Civil Rights law at all. This is because making sex a category of discrimination was added shortly before the bill was to be voted on in Congress in an effort to stop the bill from passing. But, the bill passed anyway, making sex discrimination in the workplace illegal in 1964.

Title VII makes employment discrimination based on sex illegal, but allows for "bona fide occupational qualification" exceptions, which permit an employer to establish certain requirements that employees must meet to hold a job. It covers those who apply for a job as well as employees, but only applies to employers with 15 or more workers. It also prohibits retaliation against any person who reports or assists in the investigation of sexual harassment.

SEXUAL HARASSMENT AS A FORM OF SEX DISCRIMINATION

Even though Title VII of the Civil Rights Act became effective in 1964, it wasn't until more than a decade later that a few courts were even willing to recognize sexual harassment as a form of prohibited sex discrimination.

Until the mid-1970s, courts viewed complaints of sexual harassment as "personal relationship" problems instead of discrimination.

CASE

In 1975, when two women filed suit stating that they were forced to resign from their jobs because their supervisor made repeated sexual advances towards them, the court said that it would be "ludicrous" to permit the women to proceed with a lawsuit because of their supervisor's "amorous" advances and so dismissed the women's complaint.

Some courts, however, began to recognize sexual harassment.

CASE

In 1976, a worker filed suit because her supervisor retaliated for her refusal to engage in sex with him by refusing to supervise her or to explain to her how to perform her job and then reprimanding her when she did it wrong. The employer claimed she was fired for poor work performance, and that

(continued)

> the conduct of its supervisor was "an isolated personal incident which should not be the concern of the courts." The court disagreed and said it was sex discrimination.

In 1980, the Equal Employment Opportunity Commission (EEOC), the federal agency charged with enforcing the anti-discrimination laws, issued guidelines which defined sexual harassment. This helped, because federal courts follow these guidelines. Soon after, courts began to recognize the two different types of sexual harassment.

QUID PRO QUO

Quid pro quo ("something for something") cases were the first type of sexual harassment to be recognized by the Supreme Court of the United States.

> In 1986, in the case of ***Meritor Savings Bank v. Vinson***, 477 U.S. 57, a female bank employee was sexually harassed, in and outside of work by her supervisor, who was the vice president of the bank. She had worked at the bank for four years, before she took a sick leave and was fired for failing to return to work. She filed suit and explained that she began as a teller and, based on her work performance, was promoted to assistant branch manager. During her probationary period as a teller-trainee, the supervisor had treated her much like a daughter. He made no sexual advances during that time. Later, he invited her out to dinner at which he suggested that they go to a motel and have sex. At first she refused, but out of fear of losing her job she agreed. After that, at her supervisor's repeated demands, she had sex at least 40 times over a four year period, usually at the bank, both during and after business hours. He also fondled her in front of other employees, followed her into the women's rest room,
>
> *(continued)*

CASE

exposed himself to her, and raped her on several occasions. There was also evidence that the supervisor had inappropriately touched other female bank employees. Because she was afraid of him, the victim never reported his harassment to the bank.

Like many other courts during that time, the trial judge in the above case found that she voluntarily had a relationship with her supervisor and it had nothing to do with her employment at the bank. She appealed to the federal appellate court, and it disagreed with the trial court, stating that her supervisor's demands for sex were a condition of employment and were not welcomed by her.

This time, the employer appealed, and the case went to the Supreme Court of the United States. There, the Supreme Court held that the sexual conduct was clearly not welcomed by her since she submitted to the sexual relationship for fear of losing her job. The Court said that it was "demeaning and disconcerting" for a worker to have to "run a gauntlet of sexual abuse in return for the privilege of being allowed to work and make a living." With these words, courts opened their doors to the *quid pro quo* form of sexual harassment.

The two legally required elements of a *quid pro quo* case are:
- an employee is subject to unwelcome sexual advances and
- submission to the sexual advances is a condition of a job benefit or refusal to submit resulted in a detriment.

Thus, the employee, to keep her job, was required to submit to sex or face being fired if she refused.

In addition to covering employees, it is *quid pro quo* sexual harassment if a job applicant refuses sexual demands of an employee who makes hiring decisions (or tells her that he does) and is denied the job. It may also be *quid pro quo* sexual harassment if an applicant for a job is rejected in favor of another less qualified person simply because the person hired submitted to the sexual demands of the supervisor.

Today, many of the issues have been answered in *quid pro quo* cases. Showing that there has been a "sexual advance" and demonstrating that the victim was hired, fired, demoted or otherwise actually affected is pretty straightforward, but a few issues continue to be raised in this type of sexual harassment case today. Often these include issues such as cases in which there has been a former intimate relationship or in cases of favoritism.

Former Relationship

This issue involves the question of whether the sexual acts were "unwelcome." Where there was a former sexual relationship between the parties, courts look to see how the person who complains of sexual harassment put her former boyfriend or spouse or significant other on notice that the relationship had ended and that his advances were no longer welcome. The plaintiff must have made it clear that his advances were no longer welcome.

Favoritism

This issue arises when a supervisor promotes his girlfriend to a position you were also qualified for. If the person promoted is actually his girlfriend, it will not generally be considered sexual harassment, but if there is a pattern where workers who submit to sex with the supervisor get promoted, then sex may be considered a "condition" of the job and it can be found to be sexual harassment under the law.

HOSTILE ENVIRONMENT

The second type of sexual harassment, hostile environment, was clearly recognized in 1980 with the adoption of the EEOC guidelines. In this type of case, the victim cannot show a job loss or pay cut, but the work environment is so hostile that it affects her working conditions.

Elements

Hostile environment cases are not as easy to identify as *quid pro quo* cases, because there is no exact formula that determines what constitutes a hostile environment. In the workplace, the legal elements of a hostile environment case are:
- an employee was subject to unwelcome sexual harassment and
- the harassment unreasonably interfered with the employee's work performance; or,
- the harassment created an intimidating, hostile or offensive environment.

Sufficiently Severe or Pervasive

In considering whether sexual harassment is "sufficiently severe or pervasive" so as to alter the conditions of an employee's work and create an abusive environment, courts look at all of the circumstances presented, including:
- how often the harassing conduct occurred;
- how severe the conduct was;
- whether the conduct was physically threatening or humiliating;
- whether the conduct unreasonably interfered with the victim's work performance; and,
- the presence of psychological harm to the victim.

Isolated Comments

Because the sexual harassment has to literally "change the conditions" of her environment, the Supreme Court has said that a single sexual comment or remark, even if it was obnoxious or demeaning, is not enough, by itself, to demonstrate a hostile environment. This is also why an instance of flirting, innuendo and even isolated obscenity or vulgarity will not establish the existence of a hostile environment. But it is also true that there is no clear minimum level of conduct that must be shown. For example, if a single derogatory comment is repeated by many different workers, then the conduct is no longer isolated and can be considered sexually harassing. It is also true that the more severe the harassment, the less need there is to show that it has been repeated.

Psychological Harm

The Supreme Court has made clear that a woman does not have to wait until she literally suffers mental harm before she can prove a hostile environment.

In 1993, in ***Harris v. Forklift Sys., Inc.***, the Court said that an employee who works in an environment that is poisoned with severe and pervasive sexual harassment does not have to wait until she is psychologically harmed before she can file a lawsuit under Title VII. In Harris, the Court found that where a female employee was continually mocked and ridiculed with dirty jokes, lewd comments, and sexual innuendo by the president of the company, the constant harassment made her job stressful and unpleasant and she was entitled to leave and file suit before she became injured as a result.
(510 U.S. 17 (1993).)

CASE

EMPLOYER DEFENSES

Once the plaintiff establishes her claim of sexual harassment, the employer is entitled to respond. In a *quid pro quo* case, for example, an employer may:

•disagree or

•explain that the worker was affected for a legitimate reason.

For example, the employer may explain that the decision to fire the worker was not based on her sex, but instead was based on her poor performance or absenteeism. In a hostile environment case, the employer will claim that it was:

•isolated conduct or

•even if the conduct was repeated, it was not so severe that it affected the employee's work conditions.

In both types of cases, an employer can try to show that the conduct was 'welcomed' by the plaintiff. In certain cases, the employer may also raise the defense that it had a sexual harassment policy but the victim failed to use it so it never had a chance to remedy the situation.

PRETEXT

Once the employer puts on its case, the plaintiff is entitled to argue that the decisions made were "pretextual," i.e., that it was a cover for the true motive of sexual harassment. For example, where the victim of harassment was laid off, but no one else was, a court could find that the layoff was due to the harassment or in retaliation for reporting despite the employer's argument that the layoff was because of a downturn in its business.

RETALIATION

Title VII also forbids retaliating against a person who reports or cooperates in the investigation of a sexual harassment claim. A plaintiff is entitled to protection from retaliation for making the complaint as is any worker who cooperated in the investigation of the complaint .

The elements of a retaliation case are:

- Was the worker a person who filed a complaint of sexual harassment or did the worker cooperate in an investigation of such a complaint?
- Was the employer aware that the worker it took action against was part of the sexual harassment investigation?
- What negative action was the worker subjected to?
- Was that negative action caused by the pursuing of the complaint of sexual harassment?

In one case for example, a sergeant with the sheriff's department sexually harassed a court aid under his supervision. She said he forced her to have sex with him to get favorable treatment and avoid discipline in her job. The county settled her sexual harassment suit for $450,000. But two months after she settled the lawsuit, the woman was fired. She sued for retaliation, because prior to being fired she was suspended several times, once she was even suspended for thirty days because she did not report for work on the day she gave pre-trial testimony in the sexual harassment case! This employer did not learn its lesson the first time and the county ended up agreeing to pay another $150,000 to settle the retaliation lawsuit.

CASE

In the case above, the sergeant was the plaintiff in the sexual harassment suit and despite the fact that it knew this, the sheriff's department suspended her for pursuing her claim and actually fired her in retaliation. Therefore, it was a separate violation of her civil rights. Note that this would be true even if she had not won her first case of sexual harassment. This is because the law wants to encourage workers to pursue their civil rights, even if they cannot fully prove them. If employers were allowed to fire workers hoping that they could not prove their claims, it would make it difficult for workers to take that risk and make the complaint.

REMEDIES

If an employer is held responsible for sexual harassment, the plaintiff is entitled to be restored to the position she would have been in before the harassment. These are called "make whole" remedies. The plaintiff may also be entitled to compensatory and punitive damages, attorneys fees and costs. Also, the court may order the employer to take certain actions to end sexual harassment. Remedies granted by a court will be designed to address the facts of the case presented.

Make "Whole" Remedies

These remedies are designed to restore employment losses due to the harassment. These can include:
- back pay;
- hiring;
- promotion;
- reinstatement; and,
- front pay.

Back Pay

This remedy can be ordered to restore lost wages or salary, overtime, shift pay differential, or other lost benefits such as vacation or sick leave, pension, retirement, profit sharing or other fringe benefits like medical and life insurance. The law allows back pay for up to two years prior to filing a charge with the EEOC. Back pay will terminate with the entry of the judgment in the sexual harassment case. The plaintiff does have a duty to mitigate. This means that she must actively seek to be re-employed at a comparable income, and if so, that amount will be deducted from the back pay awarded.

Hiring, Promotion, Reinstatement

The plaintiff can be hired on the terms and with the same seniority she would have had if she had been hired at the time of the sexual harassment. She may also be reinstated to the position that the sexual harassment kept her from being promoted to with all the benefits accruing from the time she should have been promoted. Also, a court can order that all negative evaluations be removed from her personnel file.

Front Pay

Sometimes reinstatement is not possible, for example, where the job no longer exists, or where it is not feasible to put the plaintiff into a particular position. Where it would be inappropriate to return to her to the job, "front pay" for a certain length of time can be ordered. Front pay is like back pay except that it applies to the future. It includes future salary or wages and benefits that she would have earned had she been returned to the position. Front pay will be ordered only until the time it is estimated that the plaintiff would get comparable work.

Injunctive Relief

The ability of a court to order a company to do or to stop doing something is especially important in hostile environment cases. For example, a court can order the company to cease the sexually harassing conduct. It can also order the company to provide training and educational programs to prevent sexual harassment. A court may also order the company to adopt, implement, and enforce a policy and procedures for the prevention and control of sexual harassment.

Attorney's Fees and Costs
Plaintiffs who win their Title VII suit can also recover attorneys' fees, expert witness fees, and court costs.

DAMAGES AND THE CIVIL RIGHTS ACT OF 1991
A plaintiff who files a lawsuit is entitled to various remedies for her injuries. In addition to the remedies discussed above, a plaintiff is entitled to money damages for sexual harassment. As it was initially passed in 1964, Title VII only provided that victims of sexual harassment could be reinstated to their job and collect back pay and lost earnings if they proved their case. But a victim of sexual harassment was not permitted to recover for her pain and suffering.

Compensatory Damages
In 1991, after the Anita Hill case, the U.S. Congress passed amendments to Title VII to allow sexual harassment victims to request a jury trial to recover money damages as compensation for their injuries. The compensation can include future money damages and recovery for emotional pain and suffering.

Punitive Damages
Where there is intentional or reckless discrimination by a private employer, the sexual harassment victim can also seek punitive damages. Punitive damages are not available against state or local governments. This type of damage award is designed to punish an employer who intentionally caused harm or who was reckless or acted with "callous indifference" to the victim's harassment.

One court identified the factors relevant to imposition of the punitive damage consideration:
- How reprehensible was the conduct?
- What are the potential civil penalties?
- Does the award serve the future goal of deterrence?

Damage Cap

The 1991 amendment expanding the right to damages, however, provides for a combined compensatory and punitive damage cap depending on the number of employees at the workplace. For example, the maximum a company employing fifteen to one hundred employees could be sued for is $50,000. Employers with 101-200 employees can face up to $100,000. For 201-500 employees, it is $200,000. And, for companies with 501 or more, the cap is $300,000.

STATE FAIR EMPLOYMENT PRACTICE LAWS

Most states, and some municipalities, have passed fair employment practice laws that bar sexual harassment. These laws are similar to the federal law, but they have differences in coverage and remedies.

Reasons for pursuing a claim under the state or local law include:
- a longer period within which to file a claim;
- coverage of smaller employers;
- the ability to charge a supervisor personally; or,
- more favorable remedies.

For example, under New Jersey state law, the plaintiff has a much longer time within which to file (six years) than federal law. And, unlike federal law, California does not put a cap on damages, so the award might be larger. Also, some states, like Iowa and Washington, hold a supervisor *personally* responsible for his or her sexual harassment, but under federal law it is the employer who is responsible. Finally, unlike federal law, which applies only to employers with fifteen or more persons, some states cover much smaller employers.

Your state agency can provide information on whether your city has a local ordinance prohibiting sexual harassment. To find your state's law and agency, look in Appendix E.

TORT ACTION

In some instances, a plaintiff who files suit under the anti-discrimination laws, can also add private claims, which might provide additional remedies. Sometimes, plaintiffs will not file under anti-discrimination laws at all, and, in such a case, there is no requirement that any claims be first filed with the anti-discrimination agency, like the EEOC. Instead, the plaintiff can go directly to court. These decisions are best made after consultation with an attorney. See Chapter 16 for more information on finding an attorney.

Torts are lawsuits that claim a wrongful act that injures another and for which the law imposes civil liability. Common claims in these lawsuits include assault and battery, defamation, false imprisonment, invasion of privacy or the tort of outrage which is sometimes called intentional infliction of emotional distress.

Assault & Battery

These actions are often brought together, but they are two distinct theories. An assault involves a threat of harm while a battery involves the actual harmful or offensive contact. This tort occurs where, for example, a supervisor or co-worker threatens harm or actually pushes or grabs the plaintiff. The damages recoverable do not have a maximum cap.

Defamation

The basis for this suit occurs when a person makes false statements to others that injure the plaintiff's reputation. The statement can be made verbally or in writing. For example, in one case after the woman worker rejected the sexual advances of her supervisor, he told other employees that she was a lesbian. In most cases, the plaintiff will have to prove that the statement harmed his or her reputation either by examining the nature of the statement itself or by showing how the plaintiff's reputation suffered as a result. Like the other torts, the damages recoverable do not have a maximum cap.

False Imprisonment

If the victim has been pinned against the wall or picked up, she might include a claim of false imprisonment which requires her to show that she was held in a location against her will by a person without authority to do so. The damages recoverable are not subject to a cap.

Invasion of Privacy

Persons have right to privacy and intrusion on the privacy of another may result in a claim of invasion of privacy. Usually this results in a claim that there was public disclosure of private facts or an unreasonable intrusion into the plaintiff's private life. Damages for this tort do not have a maximum cap, but the plaintiff must show the harm that occurred as a result of the invasion of privacy.

Outrage or Intentional Infliction of Emotional Distress

When the conduct of the defendant is intentional and outrageous and causes the plaintiff harm or severe emotional suffering, it can form the basis of a suit for intentional infliction of emotional distress. Sometimes this claim is called "outrage."

This tort is frequently joined to sexual harassment complaints. Like the other torts, damages recoverable do not have a cap. However, the facts must, "shock the conscience" or be otherwise outrageous to recover under this theory.

CRIMINAL OFFENSES

The conduct which underlies sexual harassment may extend to criminal liability for the person who commits the assault or battery. Harassing a person by telephone may be criminally charged as telephone harassment under certain circumstances. Sexual crimes may be charged for the touching, fondling and more severe sexual conduct cases. Each state's law differs, but violence should always be reported to the police.

WHEN AN EMPLOYER WILL BE HELD RESPONSIBLE FOR SEXUAL HARASSMENT

7

Employers have a duty to protect their employees from quid pro quo or hostile work environment sexual harassment from supervisors, co-workers and even nonemployers like contractors or customers. When they don't, they can be held responsible for sexual harassment.

WHO AN EMPLOYER IS

Federal law defines an employer as one who has fifteen or more workers. State fair employment practice laws vary; some states include all employers no matter how many workers, and others including employers with more than twenty workers as the minimum number to which sexual harassment laws apply. See Appendix E for your state laws.

Supervisors

In certain cases of sexual harassment by supervisors, the law holds an employer completely responsible even if the employer claims that it had no knowledge of the sexual harassment. This is called *strict liability*.

This level of responsibility is placed on the employer because a supervisor is considered to be an "agent" of the employer. This means that he or she has the authority to make certain decisions on behalf of the employer. So when the supervisor acts, it is as if the employer is taking the action. Because the employer gave the supervisor that power, the employer is held responsible for the supervisor's sexual harassment.

Employers are strictly responsible for supervisors who commit *quid pro quo* ("something for something") sexual harassment. For example, one of the powers of a supervisor might be to recommend a raise for an employee. When a supervisor obtains sexual favors in return for that raise, the supervisor acts as the company's agent in abusing the authority of the employer. Similarly, the employer is strictly liable where the victim submitted to the supervisor's sexual demands and received a raise or promotion as a result. An employer will also be held strictly liable for the supervisor's hostile work environment sexual harassment if it affects a "tangible employment decision" such as the hiring, firing, promoting, demoting, or reassigning of the victim.

WHO A SUPERVISOR IS

A supervisor is simply a person with authority over an employee. This can be one's direct boss, but it can also be a supervisor who has input into the decisions made about the employee. For example, the supervisor may be on the personnel team and participate in decisions about an employee's assignment within the company. Ultimately, because many companies use different titles for their managers, the decision of whether someone is a supervisor depends more on their job function than on their job title.

Sometimes a supervisor acts as if he has more power than he actually does. He may tell the target of his harassment that he can "put in a good word for her during company evaluations." Even if he does not actually have this power, if the victim reasonably believed that the harasser has the ability to recommend a tangible employment decision, like a raise, the employer will be strictly liable for the harassment. The law holds the *employer* responsible, because it is the *employer* that has put the supervisor in the position of authority. It is more fair to put the burden for the scope of that authority onto the employer than it is to require an *employee* to figure out what exact responsibilities a supervisor has.

A TANGIBLE EMPLOYMENT DECISION

A "tangible employment decision" includes any significant change in employment status. Usually this requires an official act of the employer which will be documented in official company records. For example, a demotion is an official act of the employer and usually it results in loss of salary, wages or benefits. Other examples of tangible employment actions include:

- hiring and firing;
- promotion, and failure to promote;
- undesirable reassignment;
- significantly more or less benefits;
- significantly more or less compensation; and,
- work assignment.

Some types of significant employment changes are obvious, like promotions, but the law also covers other less obvious changes. For example, victims of sexual harassment have reported that upon refusal of the sexual advances of a supervisor, they were reassigned to a job with no defined responsibilities and no chance for advancement. "Warehousing" an employee is considered a tangible employment action even if she keeps her salary and benefits. But if the change is merely to the title of the position, that would not generally be enough to meet the requirement that the victim suffer a tangible employment action.

Once an employee shows that the harassment by a supervisor resulted in an actual employment action, the employer must provide a non-discriminatory explanation. If, for example, the employer shows that the reason for the action was not discriminatory but instead was taken as an ordinary business decision (like downsizing), the victim will then have to prove that the employer's reasons are designed to hide the true discriminatory motive of sexual harassment. For example, in one case, the victim of sexual harassment was laid off because the company said it faced a significant reduction in workforce. But the evidence showed that the company's budget projected an increase in business and no other employees were laid-off. The employer's defense of "reasonable business necessity" was rejected.

THREATS, BUT NO ACTUAL EMPLOYMENT ACTION TAKEN YET

If a supervisor threatens to demote, for example, but does not carry out the threat, the employer may still be held responsible for sexual harassment. Similarly, a victim of hostile environment sexual harassment could still be promoted, and the employer might nonetheless be held responsible for the sexual harassment. These cases, however, will be considered under a different standard.

Unlike the *strict liability* imposed in cases of actual employment action, the law in cases where the threatened action has not yet been taken permits an employer to completely avoid responsibility or to limit its liability. The employer must demonstrate all three of the following circumstances:

- the employer had a sexual harassment policy;
- effective procedures existed to address sexual harassment; and,
- the employee failed to make a complaint.

This is because the goal of the law is to prevent and correct sexual harassment. The best way to do that is to let an employer know about it so it can be corrected. These rules mean that an employee should report their case to their employer as soon as reasonably possible.

CASES

A female lifeguard for the parks department of a city worked for a male supervisor who said he would "never promote a woman." Another supervisor told her: "Date me or clean the toilets for a year." Both supervisors frequently made lewd comments about her and other women workers. They also requested sexual favors. The city had a sexual harassment policy, but it was never distributed to the lifeguards or these supervisors. She quit and then filed a lawsuit. The court said it was a hostile environment, and the city was liable for the actions of its supervisors because it did not distribute its sexual harassment policy.
(*Faragher v. City of Boca Raton*, 524 U.S. 775 (1998).)

A female sales manager was sexually harassed by the boss of her supervisor. On one business trip, the boss invited her to the hotel lounge, and commented about her breasts, telling her to "loosen up" and that he "could make [her] life very hard or very easy" at the job. A few months later when she was being reviewed for a promotion, he reached out and rubbed her knee, and said that she might not get it because she was not "loose enough." She was promoted anyway. In promoting her, he said, "you're gonna be out there with men who work in factories, and they certainly like women with pretty butts and legs." Later, when she called with a sales request, he said he didn't have time to talk unless she wanted to tell him what she was wearing. When she called back again, he denied her request, but suggested that if she was

(continued)

> wearing shorter skirts, it would make her job "a whole heck
> of a lot easier." She knew the company had a policy against
> sexual harassment, but she did not report it because her
> immediate supervisor under the policy would have been
> required to report to her harasser. She quit and filed a law-
> suit instead. The Court said that there was a hostile environ-
> ment, but the company was entitled to show that it had a rea-
> sonable policy and it might be able to avoid liability or reduce
> damages because she never used it.
> (*Burlington Industries, Inc., v. Ellerth*, 524 U.S. 742 (1998).)

HOW AN EMPLOYER PREVENTS SEXUAL HARASSMENT

The best way to prevent sexual harassment is to have good
policy and procedures which prohibit it. The employer must
also make sure that the policy gets out to the employees and
that they employees know how to use it. For more information
on using a company policy see Chapter 9 of this book.

THE RESPONSIBILITY AN EMPLOYEE HAS
TO REDUCE HARM

An employee must make an effort to use the company policy
where it is reasonable to do so. This requirement does not
mean that at the very first sign of sexual harassment an
employee must immediately file a formal complaint, but
where it is reasonable to do so, the employee must access the
company policy. Of course, if the policy is unreasonable or
ineffective then the employee will not be held to task for
failure to access it.

For example, if the only person an employee can report to
is the very supervisor who is harassing her, it is not going to be
considered a reasonable policy. Also, if the procedures require
filing a certain form, but no one has even seen a copy of the
form in their department, then the procedures will not be

considered to be reasonable. The point is that employers should be encouraging—not discouraging—employees to report and use the process.

A Hooters restaurant manger repeatedly asked a waitress to go home or to a hotel with him and told her that he would like to take her home and tie her up. These comments were "non-stop and they were very offensive" and made her feel "like a piece of meat, degraded, violated." He also put his hand in her shorts, pulled out her panty hose, and looked down into them. Another manager, also made sexist comments such as, "if he had a wife, she would bow down to him and be sub-servient to him." Hooters had a written policy against sexual harassment which was given to all waitresses and the wait-ress had signed a copy of the policy stating that she had read and understood it. But she said she did not have any faith in the policy because although she complained once, the sexual harassment stopped briefly but then continued. She did not complain again. She was awarded $25,000 actual damages and $250,000 punitive damages, but because Hooters had made a "good faith" effort to comply with anti-discrimination laws, her $250,000 punitive damage award was eliminated on appeal.

CASE

Co-workers

For co-workers who are not supervisors, the majority of cases have been decided under a theory of hostile environment. This is because usually a co-worker does not have the power over the plaintiff to create a *quid pro quo* situation. For co-workers the employer will be held responsible for sexual harassment if the employer knew (or should have known) about the sexual harassment and failed to take immediate reasonable steps to correct the situation.

An employer can come to have this "knowledge" in two ways:
1. actual or
2. constructive—when employer *should have known*.

Actual knowledge exists:
- when the managers or supervisors know about the sexual harassment, such as where the victim files a complaint;
- if the management witnesses the harassment, such as when graffiti litters the walls,or pictures are posted on bulletin boards; or,
- if other employees complain about the harassment.

Constructive knowledge means that the employer should have known. This would exist in a situation where obscene materials existed throughout the workplace. So, even if the supervisors ignored the situation and the employer claimed that no one complained about sexual harassment, the employer *should have known* about the hostile environment.

Even if no one complains of sexual harassment, an employer has a duty to prevent it. It does not matter that the employees are willing to accept it. Once the employer knows that a workplace is hostile, it has a duty to change it.

Reasonable steps to prevent or end sexual harassment requires the employer to, for example, clean off the graffiti, send out a memo prohibiting such conduct, and remind employees that anyone caught doing it again will be disciplined. Then, if it happens again, the employer should be willing to discipline the culprit(s). The employer, in many cases, will also hold a training reminding employees of the harassment. But these are some among many measures that an employer can take. Each measure will be examined in light of the circumstances faced by the employer.

Customers and other Nonemployees

The last category of persons an employer may be held responsible for and who can create a hostile work environment are third parties. This can include vendors, contractors, clients, customers or even members of the public. Like coworkers, if an employer knew or should have known of the conduct but failed to take immediate corrective action it can be held liable for the hostile environment.

CASES

A female receptionist in a lobby was subjected to a dress code that required her to wear a revealing uniform. She was sexually harassed by customers and members of the public. She made numerous complaints about the uniform which was a poncho resembling an American flag which was so short that it revealed both sides of her thighs and buttocks. The company refused to take any action to change the uniform, and she was fired when she refused to continue to wear the outfit. The company was held responsible for the customer's sexual harassment. (*EEOC v. Sage Realty Corporation*, 507 F. Supp. 599 (S.D.N.Y. 1981).)

Hooters has a dress code for waitresses. "Hooters girls" are required to wear tight white tops and bright orange shorts. The t-shirts have the Hooters owl eyes logo across the front which looks strikingly similar to nipples. Hooters has been sued several times for sexual harassment by supervisors and managers and one 1993 case involving six waitresses was brought on the basis that the dress code invited customer harassment. The waitresses said that customers felt free to make sexual comments. Some were asked if they wore underwear. Others were asked their bra size. Others were simply asked for sex. Managers told them to tolerate it. When

(continued)

they sued, Hooters settled the case. (See "Hooters Suits Allege Climate of Harassment—Management of the Chain Say the Women Who Serve as Waitresses Are Put on a Pedestal," *Orlando Sentinel*, July 20, 1993, at C6 and "Hooters" Accord Reached, NAT'L L.J., May 30, 1994, at A8 (quoting news release that states "the terms and conditions of the settlement [of all six Minneapolis suits] are confidential and all parties are satisfied with the resolution").)

Of course, the level of control an employer has over customers or other third parties is an important consideration.

CASE

A Pizza Hut waitress was subjected to two months of sexual harassment by two customers. The customers asked her personal questions, and one of them grabbed her by the hair. When she complained, her supervisor ordered her to "waitress." After she returned, "the customer pulled her to him by the hair, grabbed her breast, and put his mouth on her breast." She quit. She was awarded $200,000 and her attorney's fees. (*Lockard v. Pizza Hut, Inc.*, 162 F.3d 1062 (10th Cir. 1998).)

INDIVIDUAL HARASSERS HELD RESPONSIBLE FOR THEIR HARASSMENT

Individual harassers have not often been held liable for their harassment under anti-discrimination laws, but they can be held responsible using other routes. Federal laws regarding sexual harassment cover "employers" so usually individual employees are not held responsible. The law is written this way so that employers will not escape their responsibility by placing all the blame (and the liability) on individual employees. Otherwise, the employer would just blame the employee, fire that person, and be able to escape their responsibility for allowing sexual harassment to continue in their workplace. Some courts today, though, are willing to hold a supervisor personally responsible along with the employer. State laws vary and some do hold supervisors personally responsible for sexual harassment.

Private lawsuits for assault, battery, intentional infliction of emotional distress and other theories, and which can be joined with those for sexual harassment, are not subject to the same limitations on who can be sued. They can be brought against any person who committed the harassment. Also, depending on the conduct the harasser may be charged criminally. See Section IV of this book for more details on those options.

WHAT YOUR EMPLOYER SHOULD BE DOING TO PREVENT SEXUAL HARASSMENT

8

An employer should take all steps necessary to prevent sexual harassment from occurring, such as affirmatively raising the subject, expressing strong disapproval, developing appropriate sanctions, informing employees of their right to raise and how to raise the issues of harassment under Title VII, and developing methods to sensitize all concerned. (EEOC Guidelines.)

All employers have a responsibility to prevent sexual harassment in the workplace. The best way to prevent sexual harassment is through strong policies and procedures and through education and training programs. An employer who is serious about preventing sexual harassment in the workplace will sensitize all its employees to the issues surrounding sexual harassment. Many are in fact adopting *zero tolerance* policies, which strictly prohibit certain sexual comments or acts.

A SEXUAL HARASSMENT POLICY

Employers should have a sexual harassment policy that clearly explains to all employees that sexual harassment will not be tolerated by any employee, supervisor, coworker, customer, contractor, or anyone else who conducts business with the employer. Strong policies encourage victims to come forward and allow the employer to take prompt action to remedy sexual harassment before it affects the entire workplace.

The policy should require any employee to report the conduct that he or she believes is sexually harassing to the designated employees.

The policy should:

•clearly define sexual harassment;

•include specific examples of unlawful behavior;

•make clear that the behavior need not be directed at any particular person; and,

•provide for confidentiality for those who report or assist in the investigation of sexual harassment.

An employer will have to share some information during the investigation of the report, but the policy should provide that information will be shared on a need-to-know only basis. The employer will keep detailed records of the reports, investigation and outcome of sexual harassment cases. The policy should be that records should be available on the same need-to-know basis.

The policy should also:

•guarantee that there will be no retaliation against the victim or any person who reported the sexual harassment;

•provide information on what legal remedies are available, such as filing a complaint with the state or federal anti-discrimination agency;

•state that the employer is committed to making a prompt, thorough and impartial investigation of the complaint;

•provide that the victim will get notice of the results;

•tell violators that they will be subject to disciplinary action and what the potential sanctions are; and,

•include follow-up procedures to ensure subsequent acts of harassment or retaliation are not occurring.

LOVE CONTRACTS

Many happy relationships and marriages come from people we meet at work. But some employers see the potential for sexual harassment in socializing. To avoid liability, they develop various policies to try to avoid lawsuits for sexual harassment, one of which is the rather silly policy of having employees sign a "love contract."

These "agreements" require the employer to state that their private sexual behavior with another employee is "welcome." The "contract" usually asks the employee to agree to *arbitration* through a fair employment agency or court. Employers who offer these agreements believe that they can head off a sexual harassment complaint which arises out of a "soured relationship."

Be aware that these "contracts" are not really a contract at all. They invade an employee's privacy and don't protect employees. Their real goal is to shield an employer from liability. If you are asked to sign such an agreement, which may also be called a "memo of understanding," you should consider speaking to an attorney about it.

More often, employers have policies that prohibit one spouse from supervising another or any person from supervising someone that they have an intimate relationship with.

COMPLAINT PROCEDURES

A sexual harassment policy must be implemented through an appropriate grievance or complaint procedure. The grievance procedure provides the actual steps for filing, investigating, and resolving reports of sexual harassment.

Reporting Methods

In order to be effective, a procedure must be able to be used. Procedures that encourage reporting are *critical* to an effective policy. The procedure should describe how the report should be made and to whom. There may be a particular form to use. The procedure should have more than one way in which a report can be made. For example, the procedure should permit a report to be:

- oral;
- written;
- in person;
- by hotline; or,
- anonymous.

The policy should also provide for the length of time within which the employer's conclusions will be made. Also, information on how to appeal the report should be included.

Time Limits

The length of time to report sexual harassment should be clearly stated in the procedures. Employers who put unreasonably short time limits for reporting sexual harassment will be found to have an unrealistic procedure. On the other hand, employers are under a duty to promptly resolve sexual harassment and they want employees to promptly report it.

The procedure should also specify the time line for investigating and resolving reports. For example, once the complaint is filed, the length of time to review records, interview witnesses and other evidence should be specified. Once the investigation is concluded, the length of time within which a written report is due should be specified, and the time and mechanism for appeal by the person who reported the harassment or the person who is accused should be specifically provided.

Interim Measures

After a complaint is reported, and while it is being investigated, the employer has a duty to protect the victim and to prevent continued harassment or retaliation for reporting. Interim measures allow the employer to temporarily correct the situation. For example, a victim can request a:

- •transfer;
- •shift change;
- •new seat assignment; or,
- •increased supervision or monitoring.

Interim measures will also allow the employer to temporarily suspend the person accused of harassment or remove that person from the work environment.

Distribution

Every employee should get a copy of the policy and procedures of the employer. These will usually be in the employee handbook, but some states also require them to be posted in various areas of the workplace. If the policy is changed, a new copy should be distributed, and some employers just send out a copy as a reminder of its policy annually.

Investigation

Employers are required to promptly investigate whether a complaint is valid and, if it is, what the appropriate remedies should be. Employers may also investigate where there is no formal complaint. Usually, personnel from the human resources or personnel office are charged with initially investigating a complaint. They first look to see whether the conduct charged meets the definition of sexual harassment. They look at the conduct and also at the context to determine whether it was "unwelcome." Next, the investigator will determine whether the employee considered the conduct offensive. All of the circumstances surrounding the complaint will be examined.

Conclusion

If the investigation shows that sexual harassment occurred, the investigator will then prepare a report and notify the reporting employee. The person who has committed the sexual harassment will be notified and disciplined according to the employer's policy. Examples of measures to correct the effects of the harassment are:

- restoration of leave taken because of the harassment;
- deletion of negative evaluation(s) in employee's personnel file that arose from the harassment;
- reinstatement;
- discipline of the harasser;
- apology by the harasser;
- monitoring treatment of the employee to ensure that she or he is not subjected to retaliation by the harasser or others in the work place because of the complaint; and,
- correction of any other harm caused by the harassment (e.g., compensation for losses).

Discipline

Most employers have general disciplinary policies, but the sexual harassment policy should include the specific potential discipline for violating the sexual harassment policy. Usually, employers will have a progressive disciplinary policy depending on the severity of the violation. For example, a reprimand may be instituted for a first time offender and relatively minor case but the procedure might include that immediate dismissal will result from more severe conduct or repeated offenses even if of a less severe nature. The following *sanctions* (disciplinary actions) should be included in a disciplinary policy:

- oral or written warning or reprimand;
- transfer or reassignment;
- demotion;
- reduction of wages;
- suspension;
- discharge;
- training or counseling of harasser to ensure that he or she understands why his or her conduct violated the employer's anti-harassment policy; and,
- monitoring of harasser to ensure that harassment stops.

EDUCATION AND TRAINING

The employer should provide intake and annual training for all workers on its sexual harassment policies and procedures. Managers and supervisory personnel will often be given additional training to recognize their responsibilities to the personnel they supervise.

SURVEYS

Periodically, employers do evaluate whether their policies and procedures are helpful to employees. They may send out surveys or questionnaires. They may also have occasional discussion sessions with employees.

HOW YOU USE THE COMPANY PROCESS

9

You may have initially tried ignoring the sexual harassment, wishing it would go away, but it hasn't. You may have tried telling the harasser to stop. You may have engaged co-workers to help you by putting pressure on the harasser to stop. But for all your actions, the harassment hasn't stopped. In fact, it may be getting worse. You have come to the conclusion that it is time to report your sexual harassment to your employer.

You have learned that your employer has a policy prohibiting sexual harassment in the workplace. You must read it and the procedures that implement the policy. It is especially important to understand the process you will be facing as you report sexual harassment to your employer. What follows is a typical process that employers engage in when responding to sexual harassment, however, every employer is free to develop individualized policies and procedures which address sexual harassment.

For example, most have fairly short time lines for reporting and investigating a complaint. Your employer has strong reasons to promptly investigate sexual harassment according to its policies. But recognize, too, that while your employer is trying to promptly resolve your complaint, it will also be developing a record for defenses that it might later raise should you make a complaint to an outside agency. One of those defenses might be your failure to promptly access the employer's sexual harassment report and investigation procedures.

PRELIMINARY CONSIDERATIONS

If you are a union member, be sure to report the harassment to your union steward who can offer support for your report. According to the National Labor Relations Act, unions must represent and aid their members in stopping sexual harassment. You may wish to have a union representative or an attorney present during some of the proceedings. While the employer may do an excellent job of responding to your report, at this point you should consider talking to an attorney regarding your options. See Chapter 16 for information on how to find a lawyer.

KEEP RECORDS

Throughout the grievance or complaint process, you should keep good records of your contacts with your employer and include the same kinds of information you are documenting regarding the actual incidents of sexual harassment.

For example, for each telephone or in-person contact you have with your company about sexual harassment you should document:
- date;
- time;
- location;
- who was present; and,
- what exactly was discussed.

This way, if your employer does not resolve your complaint satisfactorily you will have good notes to use if you decide to take your complaint to an outside agency or to court.

THE REPORT OF SEXUAL HARASSMENT

The nature of sexual harassment is necessarily disturbing and distressing, but in preparing to make your report, you must carefully consider the facts that you will include. Set aside some time away from work where you can think quietly. Before you make your report, sit down and make an outline of the incidents you wish to report. Include:
- relevant facts;
- the specific sexual conduct or acts;
- how they were unwelcome to you;
- what the impact on you has been;
- when the conduct occurred;
- what supporting information you have;
- who else was present;
- who would have information about the incidents;
- why you think they have information to share; and,
- documents or materials that support your report, such as letters, pictures, drawings, etc.

NOTE: *Make sure before you provide any materials to your employer that you make copies for yourself.*

Your employer may have a form for you to fill out. If one exists, it will usually be found in the employee handbook. If no form exists, contact one of the designated people listed in your employer's policy and procedure to initiate the complaint when you are prepared.

INVESTIGATION OF THE REPORT

Your employer will use the company's process as a guide to conducting the investigation. See the previous chapter for the typical parts of an employer's policy and procedures for responding to sexual harassment.

The investigation should begin promptly after the complaint is made. This may mean that day or certainly within a few days. In investigating a complaint of sexual harassment, employers will:

- question both parties in detail;
- seek supporting information from others; and,
- obtain various records, like personnel files or work logs.

INVESTIGATOR

Your employer's policy will determine who investigates complaints of sexual harassment. An investigator might be:

- a human resource employee;
- a personnel manager;
- a consultant;
- an outside agency; or,
- a lawyer.

Whoever the investigator is, the goal of this person should be to impartially gather all the relevant evidence to determine whether a claim of sexual harassment can be substantiated and to make recommendations about resolving the report.

The investigator should have special training in the law and employer responsibilities in sexual harassment. The investigator may meet with you and others several times if necessary over the course of the investigation to gather information. Then, the investigator will write a report and come to a conclusion which resolves the complaint and makes recommendations to the employer. Afterward, the investigator and sometimes a designated supervisor will meet separately with you and the person who has been accused of harassment to explain your employer's resolution of the complaint. The investigator will also explain to both parties that regardless of whether the complaint has been sustained or not, retaliation for making a good faith complaint is prohibited and can result in a sepa-rate investigation and separate remedies.

INTERVIEW OF VICTIM

The first thing that the interviewer will likely do when you report sexual harassment is speak to you. The interview will take place in a private setting. If your employer has no form, the interviewer will document the initial report for the company records, because it is important under the law for an employer to show that it promptly responded to the complaint.

The interviewer should begin by explaining how your employer handles a report of sexual harassment and going over the company's policy. Also, the employer's policy with respect to confidentiality should be explained.

After the introductory material is covered, the investigator will conduct an interview. The interviewer may choose to let you go through the report once without interruptions and then ask questions on the second time through. The interviewer may ask several questions on each point before proceeding, but you should be the one to provide the facts and details. Do not hesitate to correct the interviewer if he or she repeats any wrong or misunderstood information as part of a question.

While you are telling your experience of the harassment, the interviewer is listening and considering your words. Your credibility is being evaluated and the believability of your story is being weighed. Although talking about the sexual harassment may be stressful, you want to avoid rambling or giving a statement that is totally disorganized. Pace yourself, and if you feel that you are getting too agitated or upset, ask for a break, get a drink of water and count to ten. It also helps for you to have some outline or guide to follow.

The interviewer needs to get a complete statement from you and should be taking notes; some interviewers ask permission to tape your statement to be sure it is accurate. After your words are recorded on paper, you should be given an opportunity to look over your statement and make any corrections to it. You may also be asked to sign it.

The questions you will be asked depend on your fact situation, but will generally cover issues that establish whether the elements of sexual harassment are present, how the conduct was unwelcome to you, and the impact it had on you and others in the workplace. After a series of introductory questions which establish your employment location and job responsibilities, the interviewer will likely cover the following areas:

About the Harasser

These questions are designed to establish the name or identity of the person being accused of harassment and the position that person holds in relation to the company. Also, it is important to know what kind of working relationship you have with this person and whether you have had a relationship in the past, and if so, how did it end. Questions will include:
- Who committed the sexual acts or conduct?
- What is this person's position in the company?
- What kind of working relationship do you have with this person?
- Do you socialize or see each other outside of work?

About the Sexual Advances or Conduct

Your employer needs to establish the kind and level of company violation that is being reported. Is it the *quid pro quo* type of sexual harassment? Is it hostile work environment? If so, what is the frequency and severity of the conduct? The elements of sexual harassment will be established through questions such as:

- What exactly occurred or was said or done?
- When did it occur?
- Where did it occur?
- How often did it occur?
- Is it still ongoing?

About the Impact on You

It is important to know what kind of impact the sexual harassment is having on you and your co-workers. These questions are designed to ask about your immediate impact, but also to determine how the sexual advances or conduct is impacting you as a worker and the workplace as a whole. These questions will likely include:

- How did it affect you at that time?
- What did you do in response?
- How has the harassment impacted you personally?
- Has your job been affected in any way?

About Supportive Evidence

An employer will seek as much relevant information as is reasonable given the timeline for investigating the report of sexual harassment. You will be asked about who else or what else can provide information in questions like:

- Are there any persons who have relevant information?
- Was anyone present when the incident(s) occurred?
- Did you tell anyone about it?
- Did anyone see you immediately after the incident(s)?
- Did the person who harassed you harass anyone else?
- Do you know whether anyone complained about harassment by that person?
- Are there any notes, physical evidence, or other documentation regarding the incident(s)?

About Your Wishes

Part of your employer's duty is to promptly address sexual harassment. Interim measures should be appropriate to your needs in the workplace. For example, you may request to be transferred or moved or may ask for the harasser to be moved if more appropriate. The employer should try to accommodate your request within the limits of its policies. Be aware that you are protected from retaliation and should not be transferred or moved without your consent on the basis that you made the report of sexual harassment. Be sure to tell the investigator:

- how you would like to see the situation resolved;
- whether you feel secure in your work location; and,
- what would be reasonable for you while the investigation is going on.

About Other Information

An interviewer should give you several chances during the interview to provide additional information as it is triggered by the telling of your experiences. Certainly at the end of the interview there will be some general questions for this purpose. Also, you may recall more information after leaving the interview and you should contact the interviewer with that information. The questions will generally ask:

- Do you know of any other relevant information?
- Is there anyone else that the investigator should talk to?

At the end of the interview, the investigator should remind you of the time lines for the investigative process and let you know the next steps that your employer will be taking. The employer will question other persons you identified, and should explain to you what the company policy on confidentiality is with these persons. For example, if you identified a co-worker as being present for one of the incidents, the investigator will question her about that but will not likely share information about other incidents you described unless you indicated she was present for those also.

The interviewer should close the interview by reiterating your right to be protected against harassment in retaliation for making the complaint. The investigator should also tell you that the person you have identified as the harasser will be told not to engage in any kind of retaliation as a result of your complaint.

INTERVIEWING THE PERSON ACCUSED OF HARASSMENT

If you identified a specific person as your harasser, that person will be interviewed and will be given an opportunity to answer your report. The investigator should remain neutral. Do not be surprised if the accused harasser denies your charge regardless of the proof you have offered. After determining how the person knows you and what his or her relationship is to you, questions to the person accused of harassment may cover:

- What is your response to the complaint?
- What happened on that day?
- Why do you think the person making the report would make such a complaint?
- Why would they misunderstand you?
- Why would they lie?
- Are there any persons who can provide support for your answers?
- Who else might have relevant information?
- Are there any notes or other documentation regarding the incident(s)?
- Do you know of any other relevant information?

Just as in your interview, the investigator will tell the person accused of harassment that retaliation will not be permitted and that it can serve as the basis for a separate investigation and separate sanction even if the original complaint of sexual harassment is not sufficiently proven.

SEEKING SUPPORT

The investigator will also search for evidence that supports the statements of both you and the person who is accused of harassment. The employer may examine your and the harasser's personnel files to determine if there have been any prior complaints or work issues related to your complaint. The employer will also seek out other victims that may exist. You or the accused harasser may also have identified various non-employees and give permission to your employer to contact them for additional information. For example, you may have given permission to obtain medical records to document your absenteeism due to stress-related illnesses.

Your co-workers will be interviewed as well as any supervisors who may have contact with you. The employer will ask about the specific conduct if you identified them as witnesses. These persons may also be asked about your demeanor and the demeanor of the harasser. Others who have been identified as having some relevant information will also be questioned. Employers will often ask the following questions of them:

- What did you see or hear?
- When did this occur?
- What was the behavior of the person accused toward [you] and others in the workplace?
- What did [you] say about the incident(s)?
- When did s/he tell you this?
- Do you know of any other relevant information?
- Are there other persons who have relevant information?

THE INVESTIGATOR'S REPORT OF CONCLUSIONS

Once all of the necessary persons have been interviewed and all of the relevant material has been examined, the investigator will come to a conclusion on whether there is a reasonable basis to believe that sexual harassment occurred. Each employer is free to use different terms in their policies, but there are generally three categories of conclusions to a sexual harassment complaint. It can be:

1. sustained (has sufficient evidence);
2. unfounded (found to be untrue);or,
3. unsubstantiated (does not have sufficient evidence.

The investigator will weigh the credibility of the witnesses and the consistency of the statements and the existence of any documents or material that has been provided or reviewed against the elements of a sexual harassment complaint. No single statement or item will usually be conclusive. Instead, it is the totality of the circumstances that are considered when making a report.

EMPLOYER'S RESPONSE

Regardless of the outcome of the individual complaint, if the harassment involved a hostile work environment claim or there is a concern that others in the workplace were affected, your employer may:

- •send a reminder to all employees about the seriousness of sexual harassment complaints or
- •set up a training for employees in your work location or throughout the employer's facility.

Sustained Report

If the investigator concludes that the evidence in your case demonstrates that sexual harassment occurred, the investigator will then recommend sanctions or turn it over to the appropriate supervisor to do so. Your employer will look to its policies to determine what sanctions to impose against the offender and what remedies are appropriate for you. For example, if the harasser is a first time offender, and the conduct involved language or pictures, the policy may call for a warning or suspension. If the conduct involved assault, however, the report should result in him being fired. You will be informed of your employer's actions.

If, as a result of the harassment, you were denied a job benefit such as a raise or a transfer or experienced some negative event, such as being disciplined or having a negative evaluation, your employer will also attempt to remedy the situation. Your raise should be retroactive, any negative evaluation should be removed from your personnel file, and you should be returned to the position you would have been in except for the harassment.

Unsubstantiated Report

When there are key inconsistencies in the statements gathered which cannot be resolved, the employer may be unable to find sufficient support for your complaint to substantiate it. If your employer determines there is not enough evidence to sustain the complaint, it will inform you and the accused harasser of its decision.

Unfounded Report

Although it is rare, occasionally an intentionally false complaint of sexual harassment is made. If your employer determines that your complaint was made in bad faith, that is, intentionally false, your employer could discipline you for dishonesty according to its policies. However, your employer must be very careful not to engage in what might appear to be retaliation to avoid being held responsible for committing a separate violation under federal or state laws.

MONITORING

If the complaint is substantiated, it is likely that the employer will keep a file open to monitor the situation for some period of time. The employer may also periodically check with you to see if there are any more incidents or problems. Even if your employer finds the complaint "unsubstantiated" or "unproven," it may increase training or monitoring of the workplace in an effort to prevent any future sexual harassment or retaliatory conduct.

EMPLOYER RECORDS

Whatever the resolution of your report, your employer will keep a written record of your complaint, the steps taken in the investigation and the ultimate report of conclusions, including dispositions.

IF YOU DECIDE TO DROP THE COMPLAINT

An employer who has notice of sexual harassment in the workplace is required to promptly investigate and respond to it. So, while you may decide you do not wish to proceed on your complaint, your employer cannot simply stop its investigation. It must continue and seek to resolve the report under the law.

DISAGREEING WITH THE SANCTIONS IMPOSED

While you will be asked what you think would the best resolution to your complaint, it is the employer, based on the policies it has, that will decide what the appropriate remedy will be.

IF YOU ARE NOT SATISFIED WITH THE RESOLUTION

You are entitled to turn to the legal system when you have been sexually harassed. Certainly, if your employer does not resolve the situation reasonably you may file a complaint with the federal EEOC or your state fair employment practice agency (See Chapter 10), or you may file a private lawsuit. Information about your legal options can be found in Section Four of this book.

FILING A COMPLAINT WITH THE EEOC OR YOUR STATE FEPA

10

During 1999, the EEOC obtained $307.2 million in benefits for victims of sexual harassment in the workplace.

Before you can turn to the courts for recovery under employment discrimination laws, you must file a complaint with the appropriate federal, state or local fair employment agency. On the federal level, for employers with fifteen or more employees, this is the Equal Employment Opportunity Commission (EEOC). States which have anti-discrimination laws have an equivalent agency called a "Fair Employment Practice Agency" (FEPA). Some municipalities have also passed ordinances prohibiting sexual harassment; these cities also have agencies designed to implement their ordinances. Federal law does not apply to employers with less than fifteen employees, but state and local laws may apply to smaller employers. Find more information about the EEOC and your state's agency in Appendix A.

THE EQUAL EMPLOYMENT OPPORTUNITY COMMISSION

The Equal Opportunity Employment Commission (EEOC) is the federal agency charged with enforcing federal sexual harassment laws. Federal courts rely on EEOC guidelines in interpreting Title VII of the Civil Rights Act.

> The EEOC is very active in enforcing sexual harassment laws. The EEOC obtained hundreds of millions of dollars in benefits for victims through its enforcement efforts.

National Enforcement Plan

The number of cases of sexual harassment reported to the EEOC has tripled over the last decade. At any given time, it may have about 80,000 pending cases. Struggling with the increased volume of cases, the EEOC, in 1996, developed a plan which prioritizes three types of cases:

- cases in which the potential impact goes beyond the parties;
- cases which can develop the law; and,
- cases which affect the EEOC process.

This means that the EEOC will often focus its resources on larger cases. The EEOC can and does file class action suits involving numerous women at the same company who complain of sexual harassment.

CASES

In the past few years, the EEOC has settled a number of big sexual harassment and retaliation cases:
- $34 million with Mitsubishi Motor Manufacturing of America for 300 to 400 female employees.
- $10 million with Astra USA for eighty to one hundred female victims.
- $8 million with Ford Motor Company for its women workers.
- $3.2 million with Tyson Foods, Inc.

(continued)

- •$2.6 million settlement with Sidney Frank Importers and All State Promotions, distributors of Jagermeister liquor and Grey Goose Vodka for over one hundred female employees in New York State.
- •$1.9 million with Long Prairie Packing, a Minnesota-based meat packing company for men sexually harassing male workers.
- •$1.85 million with lettuce grower/distributor Tanimura & Antle, Inc. for a *quid pro quo* and retaliation case.
- • $1.3 million settlement with Foster Wheeler Constructors, Inc. for racist and sexist graffiti at a construction site in Illinois.
- •$1 million with Grace Culinary Systems and Townsend Culinary for egregious sexual harassment against twenty-two Hispanic female workers who were recent immigrants in low-wage jobs at a Maryland food processing plant.
- •$500,000 with Burt Chevrolet and LGC Management in Colorado for ten former salesmen harassed by male managers.

Even if your case does not fit one of the priority categories, a charge must still be filed with the EEOC. Smaller cases or cases that do not fit the priority plan may be referred to mediation, where the parties agree, in an effort to reach an early settlement.

Filing
A charge may be filed by mail or in person at the nearest EEOC office. The name of the victim in an EEOC claim may be kept confidential. See Appendix A for contact information.

Form

The EEOC has a form for filing the charge. It can be obtained at any EEOC office. It requires your name, address, and telephone number, and the name, address, and telephone number and number of employees of your employer. A brief description of the sexual harassment including the dates of the incidents must be provided.

Time limits

There are short time limits for filing a charge of sexual harassment. A charge must be filed with EEOC within 180 days from the date of the last incident of sexual harassment. This means the date of the harassment and not the date on which your employer completed its investigation of your complaint. The 180-day filing deadline is extended to 300 days if your state or municipality has a fair employment practices act. (See Appendix E for state-specific information.) There are very few situations in which the timeline may be extended, but if you are close, be sure to file your charge or contact an attorney immediately for review of your time to file.

Classification of Charge

Once your employer is notified, the EEOC may classify your charge as one of priority investigation if the initial facts appear to support a violation of law. When the evidence is less strong, your charge may be assigned for follow up investigation to determine whether it is likely that a violation has occurred.

Dismissal of Case

The EEOC may decide to dismiss your charge if it is unable to determine that there has been a violation of the law. But even if your charge is dismissed, a "right to sue" letter is issued which gives you ninety days in which to file a private lawsuit. See Section Five for information on filing private lawsuits.

Investigation

In investigating a charge, EEOC may make written requests for information, interview people, review documents, and, as needed, visit the facility where the alleged discrimination occurred. When the investigation is complete, EEOC will discuss the evidence with you and the employer, as appropriate.

Settlement

The EEOC can seek to settle a charge at any stage of the investigation if you and the employer agree. If the case cannot be settled, the investigation will continue.

Mediation

Where the parties both agree, mediation is an informal process where you and your employer agree to settle the issues. The EEOC currently refers about 10,000 cases every year to mediation. In the process of mediation, a neutral third party will meet with the parties to negotiate a resolution. As the EEOC notes, "Mediation gives the parties the opportunity to discuss the issues raised in the charge, clear up misunderstandings, determine the underlying interests or concerns, find areas of agreement and, ultimately, to incorporate those areas of agreements into resolutions." The EEOC's mediation program is free. The process is fairly short. Most mediation sessions are completed in a single visit in just a few hours. If mediation fails to resolve the case, the EEOC will proceed to investigating the case.

Sustaining a Case

If the EEOC finds evidence that you have been sexually harassed, it may use the remedies in Title VII to settle your case whenever possible. If your case is not resolved by the EEOC, it will give permission for the case to be taken to court in a private lawsuit by issuing a "right to sue" letter within ninety days. (See Section Five of this book for information on filing a private lawsuit.)

Determination of Insufficient Evidence

If the EEOC does not have enough evidence, it will issue a determination that says:

"Based on the Commissions' investigation, the Commission is unable to conclude that the information obtained establishes violations of the statutes."

STATE AND LOCAL FAIR EMPLOYMENT AGENCIES

Like the federal law, most states provide that a complaint must be filed under the state fair employment practice law before filing with the courts. Many states and localities have anti-discrimination laws and agencies responsible for enforcing those laws, which are called "Fair Employment Practices Agencies (FEPAs)."

Through the use of "work sharing agreements," the EEOC and the FEPAs avoid duplication of effort while at the same time ensuring that a charging party's rights are protected under both federal and state law.

If a charge is filed with a FEPA and is also covered by federal law, the FEPA "dual files" the charge with the EEOC to protect federal rights. The charge usually will be retained by the FEPA for handling. If a charge is filed with the EEOC and also is covered by state or local law, the EEOC "dual files" the charge with the state or local FEPA, but ordinarily retains the charge for handling.

The procedures vary under state laws; many follow the general procedures outlined above for the EEOC. Your state FEPA can provide you with the exact procedures for your state. A listing of your state law and agencies with contact information is found in Appendix E.

NOTE: *Unless your case is settled at the agency level, you have a right to pursue your federal and state rights by filing a private lawsuit. See Section Four for more information about lawsuits.*

SECTION THREE:

Sexual Harassment In Schools

WHAT STUDENTS
CAN DO

11

The "Spur Posse," a group of high school males, sold t-shirts at school depicting points awarded for every orgasm with a different female. Calling the girls "promiscuous," a father of a "posse" member characterized the game as "healthy teenage fun." Later, seven girls and young women filed charges against nine posse members for harassment, intimidation and gang rape. In retaliation against one of the girls, "posse" members, while on school premises, threatened to kill her, physically assaulted her and called her derogatory names. The student turned to the school which failed to discipline the "posse," but suggested transferring some of the girls. In the end, most of the "posse" received minor punishment. (See Seth Mydans, "7 of 9 California Youths are Freed in a Case of Having Sex for Points," *N.Y. Times*, p.A14 (Mar. 23, 1993) and Jill Smolowe, "Sex With a Scorecard," *Time*, p.41 (Apr. 5, 1993).)

Sexual harassment in schools is as serious (and some would say more serious) a problem as it is in the workplace. Sexual harassment in schools is not a new phenomena. But it is only recently that the Supreme Court has said that schools can be held liable for money damages for sexual harassment. Courts use many of the same principles to determine the issues when sexual harassment occurs at school as when it happens at work.

A student may be sexually harassed by a:

•teacher;

•school employee;

•student;

•team member from another school;

•visiting coach; or,

•third party, like a vendor or contractor of the school.

The dynamics of sexual harassment are the same as sexual harassment in the workplace and discussed in detail in Section One of the book. As in sexual harassment in the workplace, harassers in schools are overwhelmingly male. While teachers are harassers, most reported cases of sexual harassers in elementary and high school involved other students as harassers. Most of the harassment occurs in the public areas of school facilities—halls, classrooms, the cafeteria, or on school transportation.

Courts analyze the types of sexual harassment the same way as sexual harassment in the workplace. For example, if a teacher or other school employee in a position of authority makes sex a required condition of a class or grade or other educational benefit, it is considered the *quid pro quo* form of sexual harassment. Similarly, a *hostile environment* can be caused by the sexual harassment of teachers, students, or third parties. (See Chapter 2.)

Several factors are examined, including:
- the conduct itself (nature, type, how often, for how long and where the conduct occurred);
- the persons involved (age and sex of the student and alleged harasser, the number of alleged harassers and/or whether an alleged harasser was in a position of power over the student);
- whether the conduct adversely affected the student's education or educational environment; and,
- the existence of other incidents of sexual harassment at the school.

WHAT THE LAW SAYS

Sexual harassment of students is prohibited by Title IX of the Education Amendments of 1972. Under Title IX, no individual may be discriminated against on the basis of sex in any education program or activity receiving federal financial assistance. Title IX applies to all public and private schools that receive federal funds, i.e., recipients, including, but not limited to, elementary and secondary schools. Sexual harassment of students is a form of prohibited sex discrimination.

The United States' Department of Education's Office of Civil Rights (OCR) is responsible for enforcing Title IX. About 14% of the more than 6,600 complaints OCR received in 1999 involved sex discrimination. Sexual harassment has a high priority in OCR and it is committed to ending sexual harassment in schools because it recognizes that "sexual harassment can interfere with a student's academic performance and emotional and physical well-being." Eliminating sexual harassment can help students learn in a safe school setting.

Title IX protects both male and female students from sexual harassment by a school's employees, other students, or third parties. Also, it covers any school activity. So students are entitled to be free from sexual harassment in the classroom, after school activities, the bus, or at any school sponsored event.

Schools can be held liable for money damages for teacher on student sexual harassment if the school or school board:

•knew or should have known of the conduct;

•had the power to end the abuse; and,

•failed to do so.

CASE

A female high school student, alleged that when she was a sophomore and over the course of two years, an athletic coach and teacher forcibly kissed her in the school parking lot, telephoned her at home, engaged her in sexually explicit conversations, and interrupted one of her classes to take her to a private office where he subjected her to "coercive inter-course." School officials, aware of this behavior, investigated the matter but failed to take action to protect her. In fact, the school district even discouraged her from reporting to the authorities. The Supreme Court found the school district liable for sexual harassment. (*Franklin v. Gwinnett County Public Schools*, 503 U.S. 60 (1992).)

The Court, a few years later, said that damages were only appropriate when school officials had actual knowledge and failed to adequately respond. If the school does have notice and fails to take reasonable steps designed to end the harassment, it will be considered to be deliberately indifferent and liable.

> Where a teacher of a ninth grader made sexually suggestive comments, and later kissed and fondled her while visiting her at home and engaged in sexual intercourse throughout a two year period, the school would not be held liable. As soon as the school was officially notified that the teacher was arrested, the school fired him. (*Gebser v. Lago Vista Independent School District*, 524 U.S. 274, 290 (1998).)
>
> **CASE**

More recently, the Supreme Court has determined that student-on-student sexual harassment is also prohibited as unlawful.

> A fifth grader was harassed by a classmate for months. She stated a claim for sexual harassment where the school knew about it but responded by asking why she "was the only one complaining." It took 3 months for the school to even change the victim's seat so she would not have to sit next to her harasser.
> (*Davis v. Monroe County Bd. of Ed.*, 526 U.S. 629 (1999).)
>
> **CASE**

THE SCHOOL'S RESPONSIBILITIES 12

Schools have a responsibility to prevent sexual harassment. But they also must exercise common sense in determining whether a behavior constitutes sexual harassment. Because the law applies equally to kindergarten and graduate schools, school personnel must consider the age and maturity of students in responding to allegations of peer sexual harassment. For example, if a first grader kisses another on the cheek, this should not be considered sexual harassment.

MEASURES TO PREVENT SEXUAL HARASSMENT

The best way to prevent sexual harassment in schools is to prevent it from getting started. The school policy should:
- state the school's commitment to eliminate harassment;
- clearly define the types of harassment;
- include examples of the kinds of harassing behaviors covered;
- identify the locations and activities covered;
- explain how the school will investigate harassment;
- discuss the possible resolutions;
- provide reporting contacts;
- list the methods by which a report can be made; and,
- prohibit retaliation against persons who report harassment or cooperate in the investigation of a report.

RESPONDING TO HARASSMENT

When schools learn about sexual harassment, they must promptly investigate and take action to end the harassment. Schools can be held responsible to pay money damages to victims of sexual harassment if they know about the harassment and fail to take immediate, effective action to end it. A school can learn about harassment from a report by a victim or from any employee who is required to report it. But a school may also be held to know about it if there is obvious graffiti or written material or if it is reported in the newspaper.

MAKING A REPORT

Most schools allow reports of the harassment to be made in more than one location. Many have a form to fill out to make a report.

PROCEDURES FOR INVESTIGATING REPORTS

Schools are required by the Title IX regulations to have grievance procedures through which students can complain of sexual harassment. Once a school is on notice that sexual harassment occurred, it must take prompt and effective action calculated to end the harassment, prevent its recurrence, and, as appropriate, remedy its effects. Most schools have procedures in place to investigate all types of civil rights violations. Most also have staff and student discipline policies.

Interview

Upon receiving a report depending on the age of the victim, the parents will be notified. The appropriate personnel will then interview the victim and take a report. Then the person(s) accused of harassment will be interviewed as well as any other student, teacher or person who may have seen or heard something related to the report.

Report

After an investigation, the school will prepare a report with recommendations for resolving the harassment or closing the case due to insufficient information. Privacy concerns may limit the information given to a victim about the sanctions taken against a harasser, but the victim should be informed as to the measures the school has taken to prevent further harassment.

INTERIM MEASURES

Schools must take necessary action to prevent future sexual harassment. In the case of violence, school personnel may be required by law to report the incident to police.

Protection of the victim from continued exposure to harassment may mean separating the victim's classes or housing from the harasser where she requests it or monitoring of the victim's classes and activities within the school. It may also mean transferring the harasser out of classes, excluding him from school activities or even changing his school. All of these measures can be immediate if necessary under the circumstances, pending the results of the school's investigation.

INFORMAL COMPLAINTS

Because a school has a responsibility to investigate, a school will respond to all reports even if the victim does not want it reported or pursued.

CONFIDENTIALITY

Schools will respect student's wishes regarding confidentiality, but cannot ensure it. This is because the release of the student's name or other identifying information may be necessary to fulfill the school's obligation to investigate the report. Factors that schools consider include the age of the student, the seriousness of the harassment, the possibility of harm to the student or others, whether there are other victims, and the rights of the accused harasser.

PERMANENT RESOLUTION

Many of the interim measures may become permanent at the conclusion of the school's investigation. But a school must also right the harm that has been done to the victim. So, for example, if a bad grade was given by a harassing teacher in retaliation for the student's refusal of the teacher's sexual advances, the school should give the student an opportunity to retake the course without charge and remove the information on the bad grade from the student's grade record.

The permanency goal of the school is to end the sexual harassment. Toward that end, the school may also required additional training for students and faculty.

You may also choose to file a complaint with the agency required to enforce the federal law prohibiting sexual harassment in schools. (See the next chapter for more information on this alternative.) If you choose to file a private lawsuit, see Chapter 14.

FILING A COMPLAINT WITH OCR

13

The Office for Civil Rights (OCR) in the U.S. Department of Education is responsible for enforcing the federal statute that prohibits sex discrimination in education programs and activities that receive federal financial assistance.

WHO FILES

A complaint of discrimination can be filed by anyone who believes that an education institution that receives federal financial assistance has sexually harassed someone. It is not a requirement that the person or organization filing a complaint be the actual victim of harassment, because a complaint may be made on behalf of that person.

PROCEDURES

A complaint of sexual harassment at school may be made by contacting the Department of Education, Office for Civil Rights (OCR). The complaint can be made by filing a written document on line, by mail, fax or in person.

What to File

OCR has a form that it uses. It is available online. See Appendix B for the website. The complaint must include:
- your name, address and phone number;
- the name, address and phone number of the person filing the complaint (if different than the victim);
- the name and address of the school that is being charged with sexual harassment;
- the relationship of the victim to the school;
- a short description of the basis of the complaint of sexual harassment including the dates, names of persons involved or who witnessed the harassment; and,
- the most recent date of the sexual harassment.

Where to File

If a student or a student's parent or other representative decides to file a complaint with OCR, the complaint should be filed with the OCR enforcement office responsible for the state in which the school is located. See Appendix B for information on contacting OCR.

When to File

The complaint should be filed within 180 days of the last act of alleged discrimination. There are certain circumstances in which OCR will extend the time for filing, but you must check with OCR to be sure that they will permit an extension. For example, where a student files a grievance under school procedures within 180 days of the last act of harassment, OCR may accept the same complaint up to sixty days after the end of the grievance process.

Preliminary Screening

Once OCR receives the complaint, it will acknowledge receipt of the complaint and begin an initial review of the complaint. First, OCR will determine if it has the power to investigate the complaint. Questions that it must resolve are whether the complaint:

- •meets the definition of sexual harassment;
- •is timely (which usually means filed within 180 days);
- •is filed against a federally funded school;
- •can be resolved without further investigation; and,
- •requires more formal enforcement.

Additional Information

In resolving these questions, OCR may contact the person who filed the complaint. Additional information needed may include:

- •a written explanation of what has happened;
- •additional addresses or contact information for the complainant;
- •identifying information regarding the victim or school; and,
- •additional facts and dates.

For example, in some cases, it is necessary to identify the victim of the sexual harassment in order for OCR to investigate the complaint. If so, OCR will require a consent form be signed by the victim or by a parent or guardian before proceeding.

Until OCR receives the written consent, it cannot release the victim's name. OCR will keep the identity of complainants confidential except to the extent necessary to carry out the purposes of the civil rights laws, or unless disclosure is otherwise required by law. Information requested by OCR must be provided promptly, usually within 30 days, so that OCR does not close its file for lack of information.

Closure or Transfer of File

If OCR determines it is not the type of complaint that it has jurisdiction over, or that it cannot proceed with an investigation of the complaint because it is insufficient, then it will close its file and notify the person who filed the complaint. If OCR determines that the complaint is within the jurisdiction of another agency, it will refer the complaint to that agency.

Early Resolution

If OCR determines it has the power to investigate the complaint, it may facilitate a resolution between the parties or make an agreement that resolves the complaint. A resolution between the parties is a form of mediation in which the parties informally agree to settle the complaint.

INVESTIGATION

In investigating a report of sexual harassment, OCR will consider whether the school has a policy prohibiting sex discrimination that has been distributed, whether the school appropriately responded to the report, and whether the school has taken immediate and effective corrective action in response to the harassment. If so, OCR will close the case, but may continue to monitor any agreement it has with the school.

In the investigation phase, OCR will request documentation or records from the school and follow up with interviews of the person who filed the complaint, witnesses and school personnel. OCR will also conduct interviews of all parties. The interviews will be conducted individually, and counsel or a representative may be permitted to be present. If a witness is under eighteen, a parent's consent to interview will be sought, and the parent may be invited to sit in on the interview by OCR. A tape recording of the interview may be made with the consent of the person being interviewed.

SETTLEMENT

Whenever possible OCR attempts to settle sexual harassment complaints. This may be through informal mediation where the parties work out an agreement or it may involve the school agreeing to resolve the complaint acceptably.

OCR FINDINGS AFTER INVESTIGATION

If OCR is unable to achieve a voluntary settlement, then it will initiate enforcement to terminate federal funding or refer the case for prosecution by the Department of Justice or for other legal proceedings. OCR will issue a letter of findings which describes the findings of fact and the legal basis for the violation.

RETALIATION

The law prohibits any federally funded educational institution from retaliating against any person who has filed a complaint with OCR or who has participated in an investigation of a complaint. If you have been intimidated or retaliated against for cooperating in the investigation of a sexual harassment complaint, you are entitled to file a complaint with OCR.

APPEAL TO OCR

If you disagree with OCR's resolution of your complaint, you can contact the OCR Office Director in writing. Be as specific as possible and focus on factual or legal questions that might change the resolution of the complaint.

NOTE: OCR *will not represent the complainant in court, but a private civil lawsuit may be filed regardless of OCR's findings. (See Section Four for information on filing a complaint in court.)*

SECTION FOUR:

Legal Remedies for Sexual Harassment

FILING A LAWSUIT

14

An employment discrimination lawsuit costs at least $50,000 and takes two and one-half years to resolve.
(Baxter, Arbitration or Litigation for Employment Civil Rights 2 Ind. Employment Rights 19 (1993-94).)

What follows is an overview of the various methods by which a sexual harassment suit can be filed. Because of the complexity of these suits, and because employers and schools will have attorneys, you should consult with an attorney about the procedures involved given your facts and circumstances. Remember that an attorney's fee can be ordered paid by the employer, and a court may appoint an attorney in a Title VII case based on your ability to pay, the merits of the case and your capacity to present your own case. See Chapter 16 on the role of an attorney.

Sexual harassment can become the subject of a private civil lawsuit in one of three ways. It can be filed as a federal sexual harassment suit under Title VII (for employers) or Title IX (for schools). It can be filed as a violation of state fair employment practice acts. Or, it can form the basis for a tort action. See Chapter 10 for a discussion of EEOC suits and settlements.

These private lawsuits follow the same process as other civil suits:

1. A complaint is filed.
2. The employer or school responds to the complaint.
3. The parties obtain relevant information about each other in a process called discovery.
4. During this time, mediation may be available in an effort to reach a settlement or the parties may be negotiating on their own informally.
5. If no settlement is reached, the case goes to trial.
6. The parties call their witnesses and provide their evidence.
7. The judge makes a ruling.
8. If the judge finds for the plaintiff, various remedies can be ordered.

TITLE VII CASE

In order to file a Title VII case in federal court, a plaintiff must obtain permission from the EEOC. (See Chapter 10 for an overview of EEOC agency procedures.)

The EEOC will give this permission in one of two ways. First, after the EEOC process is completed and the case is closed, a victim of sexual harassment has ninety days after receiving a notice of a "right to sue" from EEOC, within which to file a lawsuit under Title VII. Second, a plaintiff can request a notice of "right to sue" from EEOC 180 days after the charge was first filed with the Commission. In some courts, the plaintiff will be permitted to file a lawsuit within ninety days of receipt of the "right to sue" letter even if the EEOC has not finished its investigation. Some plaintiffs do this because of the *backlog* at the EEOC, which is estimated to be tens of thousands of cases awaiting resolution.

The first civil suits brought on behalf of sexual harassment victims were all *quid pro quo* cases, such as where a supervisor demands sexual favors of a worker he supervises as a condition of getting or keeping a job benefit. The plaintiff must prove that the sexual advances were unwelcome and that it was because she rejected or submitted to the sexual advance or demand that some condition or term of her employment was affected.

The second, and by far the most common type of civil suits for sexual harassment involves victims who are subjected to a hostile work environment. Typically, the scenario for this type of case is that a co-worker or several of them engage in severe sexually harassing conduct or conduct which is pervasive and harmful and which causes the work place to be intimidating, hostile, or offensive. Again, the plaintiff must show that the defendant's conduct was unwelcome in the workplace.

TITLE IX CASE

Title IX permits a victim of sexual harassment to file a private lawsuit. Unlike the law that governs workplace harassment, Title IX does not require you to file with OCR prior to filing a case in Federal court. A private lawsuit may also be filed regardless of OCR's findings. If a complaint was pending with the OCR, it will stop its processing of a complaint once a court case is filed.

The cases borrow heavily from analysis of Title VII and utilize the same kinds of damage remedies. Many more cases of employment discrimination exist, and like Title VII cases, the most common type of case filed is rapidly becoming peer harassment cases of hostile environment.

It is also important to note that while an individual employee is not subject to a lawsuit under Title VII, an individual teacher could be sued under federal law. (U.S. C., Title 42; Section 1983.) This section allows claims against persons who deprive statutory or constitutional rights while acting with authority of the law.

THE REASONABLE PERSON STANDARD

In whose eyes will a case be judged? Most courts use a reasonable person standard—what a reasonable or average person would do under the circumstances—to determine whether the plaintiff has established her case. The EEOC guidelines suggest that this standard "should consider the victim's perspective and not stereotyped notions of acceptable reasonable person standard behavior."

PAST SEXUAL HISTORY OF THE PLAINTIFF

In an effort to show that conduct was "welcomed," the employer may attempt to discover and use the past sexual history of the plaintiff. Federal courts have frowned upon this. The Federal Rules of Evidence govern what type of evidence is admissible in a lawsuit. The federal rules protect plaintiffs privacy by protecting their prior sexual history.

For instance, one court said "a person's private and consensual sexual activities do not constitute a waiver of his or her legal protections against unwanted and unsolicited sexual harassment."

Another federal court has noted that:
"whether a sexual advance was welcome, or whether an alleged victim in fact perceived an environment to be sexually offensive, does not turn on the private sexual behavior of the alleged victim, because a woman's expectations about her work environment cannot be said to change depending upon her sexual sophistication." (Wallace v. Spucci, 217 F.3d 157 (2nd Cir. 2000).)

Some states also provide protection, but many do not because their statutes only protect victims in criminal sexual assault cases not civil sexual harassment cases. There are exceptions. California, for example, only allows the past sexual history of the victim with the offender.

PSYCHIATRIC EXAM

Courts have limited inquiry into the victim's mental state on the basis that simply because a plaintiff seeks recovery for sexual harassment does not mean that her thoughts are at issue. So, ordinarily an employer does not have a right to force the plaintiff to take a mental or psychiatric exam. However, if the plaintiff seeks damages for her mental injuries, such as in a claim of intentional infliction of emotional distress, the employer defendant is entitled to get copies of the records from a psychiatrist, psychologist or counselor.

REPEAT OFFENDERS

Some courts permit evidence to be introduced that the harasser had harassed other women in the workplace. This is important because the surveys show that many harassers are repeat offenders. This type of evidence is important to show that the harasser's purpose was not innocent or the conduct was not accidental. It establishes that the harasser has chosen to engage in the conduct on prior occasions or with similarly situated workers.

THE HARASSER CAN SUE

Harassers can sue. Most sue for improper discharge. But, generally courts are not sympathetic to their claims and find that the employer had a valid reason for the discharge.

A worker discussed with a co-worker an episode of *Seinfeld*, in which Jerry Seinfeld could not remember the name of a woman he was dating, except that the woman's name rhymed with a female body part. He asked his co-worker to guess which one it was. He even copied a page of a dictionary with the term. The co-worker, embarrassed by the discussion, made a formal complaint of sexual harassment that

(continued)

CASE

CASE

resulted in the firing of the jokester. The terminated "harasser" sued and won a $26 million dollar judgment, including a $1.5 million dollar judgment against the woman who complained! Both judgments were overturned on appeal. It turns out that the terminated worker had been warned about using sexually explicit language in the past and the company even had to pay out a prior judgment due to his conduct.

However, at times the employer does not follow its own policies and can be held liable to an employee it fired for sexual harassment.

CASE

An employer who fired a worker for sexual harassment was ordered to pay $40,000 in lost wages where it violated its own disciplinary policies. The employer was also ordered to pay the man's attorney's fees.
(*Jesso v. Letica Corp.*, 2000 Mich. App. LEXIS 2812 (Mi.App.2000).)

Courts that have been faced with an individual who was accused with harassment that sued his accuser have determined that no claim was stated.

SECTION FIVE:

The Law and Lawyers

LEGAL RESEARCH

15

Laws can be found in statutes or codes of both the federal and state government. The federal and state laws are found in the codes which are listed in the Appendix. To find your laws, you will need to do some basic legal research.

STATUTES OR CODES

A large public library may carry some legal books, but a specialized law library will have the most up-to-date version of the governmental codes as well as other types of research materials not found in a regular public library. Law libraries can usually be found at or near the local courthouse—your court clerk's office should be able to tell you where to find the law library. Also, any law school will have a law library.

Contact the closest law library to determine hours and directions. Ask if there are any restrictions on the use of the library by members of the general public. Some law libraries may have limitations (such as limited hours or days) for non-attorneys. Law school libraries may have similar (or stricter) restrictions for non-students.

Your first step will probably be to find the basic law in the federal and state statutes or codes. The actual title of the set of books containing the statutes or codes is very important.

Refer to the listings in the Appendix to find the title of the appropriate books. Reference librarians are also very good and can help you find the set of books you are looking for. Once you find the proper set of books, look for the section, title, or other numbers listed in the Appendix in order to find the exact provisions of the laws.

For example, if you are looking at the listing in the Appendix for the Title VII of the United States Civil Rights Act, which is the federal statute that prohibits sexual harassment in employment, you will see the following notation after the heading "The Law": United States Code, Title 42, Section 2000e. (42 U.S.C. § 2000e). This gives you the title (42) and Section (2000e) of the set of books (United States Code).

NOTE: *The U.S. Code also comes in two "annotated" versions called the United States Code Service (U.S.C.S.), and the United States Code Annotated (U.S.C.A.). The U.S.C.S. and U.S.C.A. versions of the statutes contain helpful notes and references to make them easier to use.*

As you continue to look at the appendix information for the federal statute, you will also note the following notation under the heading "Scope": 2000e. This tells you that the portion of the law relating to who is a covered employer for purposes of the Civil Rights Act is found at Section 2000e of Title 42 of the United States Code. The legal citation for this section would be 42 U.S.C. §2000e. (The symbol "§" means "Section.")

Similarly, if you look at the listing for Illinois in the Appendix, you will see the following notation after the heading "The Law": West's Illinois Compiled Statutes Annotated, Chapter 775, Article 5, Section 1-101 (775 ILCS 5/1-101). This gives you the title (775) and Section (5/1-101) of the set of books (West's Illinois Compiled Statutes Annotated). You will also note the following notation under the heading "Scope": 5/2-101. The Illinois Human Rights Act is found at Chapter 775 of the Illinois Compiled Statutes in Article 5 at section 2-101. The legal citation for this section would be 775 ILCS 5/2-101.

Once you locate the specific laws, check to see if there is a more current version available. This may be in the form of an update in the back of the volume, a separate update volume, or in some other format. If necessary, ask a reference librarian for assistance in order to be certain you have the most recent version. The statutes may also be annotated with short summaries of court decisions which have interpreted the statutes.

CASE REPORTERS

There are federal case decisions that have interpreted the federal sexual harassment statutes. Your state courts may also have interpreted your state's laws. If you wish to find the court's entire opinion, it will be included in the federal, state or regional case reporter.

The federal case reporters contain court opinions from the federal courts. Cases from the United States Supreme Court appear in United States Reports (U.S.), in the Supreme Court Reports (S.Ct.), or in the Lawyers' Edition (L.Ed.). Cases from the federal courts of appeal appear in the Federal Reports (F.) which has a second (F.2d) and is currently in the third series (F.3d). Cases from the federal trial courts appear in the federal supplement (F.Supp.) reporters.

A state *case reporter*, such as the Illinois Reports, contains court opinions from the courts of a single state. A *regional reporter*, such as the Northeastern Reports, contains cases from the courts of several states in a certain geographic area.

To find a case, carefully copy down the case name and the numbers which follow it (called the citation), or make a copy of the page with the case information. Next, locate the "case reporters" in the library. Ask your reference librarian for assistance.

For example, the United States Supreme Court's cases may be found in either the United States Reports or in the Supreme Court Reports as follows:

Burlington Industries, Inc. v. Ellerth, 524 U.S. 742, 118 S.Ct.2257 (1998)

| NAME | UNITED STATES | PARALLEL | YEAR |
| OF CASE | REPORTER | REPORTER | PUBLISHED |

Once you find the proper federal reporter, the citation is found using the following method:

| 524 | U.S. | 742 |
| VOLUME | REPORTER | PAGE NUMBER |

Thus on page 742 of volume 524 of the United States Reports case reporter you should find the Supreme Court's opinion in Burlington Industries, Inc. v. Ellerth, which was decided in 1998.

Many states have more than one reporter in which the same case can be found. The stated citation often looks as follows:

State v. Human Rights Comm'n, 178 Ill. App. 3d 1033, 534 N.E.2d 161 (4th Dist. 1989)

| NAME | STATE CASE | REGIONAL | YEAR |
| OF CASE | REPORTER | REPORTER | PUBLISHED |

Once you find the proper state or regional reporter, the citation is found using the similar method as detailed on the previous page:

178 Ill.App.3d 1033

| VOLUME | STATE COURT | SERIES VERSION | PAGE NUMBER |

Thus on page 1033 of Volume 178 of Illinois Appellate 3d series case reporter you should find the appellate court opinion in *State v. Human Rights Comm'n*, decided in 1989 by the fourth district appellate court. After a point, instead of continuing to increase the volume numbers, publishers have started over with volume one of a subsequent series of the reporter. In our example, you would actually find three series of books on the library shelves: one titled Illinois Appellate Reports; another titled Illinois Appellate Reports, Second Series (2d), and a third titled Illinois Appellate Reports, Third Series (3d). Each set begins with 'Volume I.' The Third Series contains the most recent cases.

INTERNET RESEARCH

Increasingly, the Internet is becoming a resource to obtain legal information. The federal government and many states include their statutes and selected cases on their government web pages. For example, the Equal Opportunity Employment Commission (EEOC) maintains a website at **www.eeoc.gov** as does the Office for Civil Rights at **www.ed.gov/Offices/OCR**. These contain helpful information and explanations about sexual harassment.

Searching the Internet is based on URLs (Uniform Resource Locators), also known as "web addresses" or by using key words. An easy way to find legal information is by typing in "Google.com." Another easy way to find available web information on the laws is by searching the lawcrawler search engine by Findlaw. Type in **http://www.Findlaw.com**, then choose either federal or state cases and codes to search for the appropriate information.

Researching on the Internet can be much faster than looking up the federal or state laws in the books, but online research produces only a screen snapshot at a time, so you may need to open several pages to see the whole set of laws you are seeking. When working online, be sure to review all of the relevant website information, then download or print the portion of the law in which you are interested. Then, check to see if the law has been updated or revised by checking for a *pocket part* or *supplement*.

LEGAL ENCYCLOPEDIAS

You should also be able to find sets of books called legal encyclopedias at a law library. These are similar to a regular encyclopedia, in that you look up the subject (sexual harassment) and it gives you a summary of the law on that subject, along with citations to court cases which relate to that subject. There are two national legal encyclopedias: one is American Jurisprudence (abbreviated Am. Jur.) and the other is Corpus Juris Secundum (abbreviated C.J.S.). Many states have their own legal encyclopedias such as Florida Jurisprudence (Fla.Jur.) and Texas Jurisprudence (Tex. Jur.). Like the case reporters, these may also have a second series.

DIGESTS

Another type of book found in law libraries is called a digest. Like a legal encyclopedia, you look up the subject and instead of giving you a summary of the law, it gives you summaries of court cases discussing that subject of the law. A national digest exists, and for states, search for a digest specific to your state. For example, California Digest. Again, there may be a second series.

FORM AND PRACTICE GUIDES

All law libraries have certain form and practice manuals that include the law, procedures and forms used in the federal or state jurisdiction. These can be most helpful in preparing forms or finding forms. Never hesitate to ask a reference librarian for assistance in finding a practice guide in the law library.

THE ROLE OF LAWYERS

16

Cases involving sexual harassment are considered *civil cases* (as opposed to criminal ones.) This means that a victim of sexual harassment will have to get and pay for a lawyer themselves. In some cases, though, there are legal aid clinics and law school programs, which can provide free or at least low cost legal assistance.

It is up to you to decide if you want or need a lawyer, but before you decide to make any major changes in your workplace, talk to a lawyer, and if you decide to file a complaint with a federal or state agency or decide that a private lawsuit is necessary, at the least you should consult with a lawyer to consider all of your options.

As you are evaluating your options with a lawyer, the lawyer is likely evaluating your case. Lawyers decide whether to take cases based on a number of factors, including the costs, time and effort, and their potential for collection of fees.

LAWYERS AND CONFIDENTIALITY

To encourage people to speak freely to their lawyers, the law provides confidentiality protection for clients. This is called the *attorney-client privilege*. The privilege prevents a lawyer from disclosing your information under most circumstances, so be honest in disclosing all the facts surrounding your employment, even those facts which are embarrassing or humiliating. The lawyer will need this information to properly evaluate the case.

FINDING A LAWYER

The search for a lawyer can take some time and no small amount of perseverance. Just as there are specialities in other professions, it is becoming rarer today to find a lawyer that has a general practice. The lawyer you choose should have experience in cases similar to yours.

Recommendations from Friends

Many times a lawyer is contacted on the strength of recommendations by family or friends. These recommendations can be helpful because the good experience of your family member or friend may provide reliable information on the quality of service provided by the lawyer.

Referral Services

If you do not personally know a lawyer and do not have a recommendation from a trusted friend or family member, you can look to other sources. In most cities there is a local "bar association" which is an organization to which many local attorneys will belong. The bar association can help make lawyer referrals, either formally or informally. Sometimes lawyers may list their practice in the yellow pages of the phone book under "Lawyer" or "Attorney." Some may advertise or you may read about a lawyer's representation of another sexual harassment case in the paper or see something about it on television.

Prepaid Legal Plans

If you are covered by a prepaid legal plan, check to see whether a consultation for an employment-related issue is covered.

Website

Another new area to search for finding a lawyer is on the Internet. Some lawyers now have Web pages and list their services and contact information. Even if you do not have access to the Internet at home, most public libraries now have Internet computers now for use by library patrons.

Legal Clinics

In larger populations, there are often legal clinics that provide lower-cost legal representation in employment matters. Some low-income persons may also qualify for free legal representation.

Law Schools

Some law schools maintain clinical programs which take cases. Be sure to check with any area law schools to see if any programs exist and whether your case would be eligible for service. If the clinic does accept your case, you might not be required to pay or you might have to pay on a sliding fee scale.

Attorney Registration

Every state maintains a registration of lawyers who practice law within that state. To find the phone number and address of any lawyer within your state, contact the bar association or other attorney registration office within your state. To find your local bar association, simply look in the telephone yellow pages under "lawyer referrals."

INITIAL CONTACT

The selection of a lawyer usually begins with a phone call. In this first contact with the lawyer, be sure to obtain some preliminary information and write it down as you collect it. Does this lawyer charge for a consultation? How long will the first meeting be? How much does the lawyer usually charge for his or her services? Compare the answers given by the lawyers you speak to, then decide which one to meet with for an initial consultation.

FIRST INTERVIEW

The first interview with a lawyer is very important. Remember that you have not agreed to anything other than the terms of the initial visit. Do not be intimidated by the thought of meeting with the lawyer. You are under no obligation to sign or agree to anything at this time, and you can take any written documents home to think about before you sign. Also, be sure to write down any information you obtain from the lawyer you speak to. It will help you remember who said what later.

Follow your instincts, and trust your evaluation of the lawyer when you meet. Do you like this lawyer? Do you feel that he or she is listening to you and your situation? Are you treated with respect during your visit by the office staff? Your intuition will tell you much about whether you wish to proceed further with this lawyer.

In telling the lawyer about your case, be as clear and concise as possible. You will want to bring relevant documents that will help the lawyer to understand the facts of your case.

Discuss what the lawyer thinks the projected costs will be and how you will be billed for those costs.

FEE ARRANGEMENTS

In some types of discrimination cases, attorneys charge hourly fees in addition to the expenses of the case. Most attorneys are expensive, charging more than $100 per hour, and may require a substantial initial payment (sometimes called a "retainer") from you to begin the case (although a court may order the wrongdoer to pay for your attorney's fees when you win).

If a retainer is to be paid, make sure that you and your lawyer agree what minimum services are to be provided for that sum. For example, for a retainer of $500 or more, the lawyer should at least prepare and file your complaint and have the employer, school, or defendant served. What you want to avoid is a situation where you pay your lawyer a retainer, he or she writes a letter and makes a few phone calls to the other side's attorney, then tells you the retainer is used up and more money is required from you to continue your case.

In sexual harassment cases that are brought under the federal statutes and some state's statutes, attorney's fees can be ordered to be paid by the employer if you are successful in your case. It may also be possible to have certain costs, such as out of pocket expenses, postage, faxes, copies, long distance calls and travel for your attorney, paralegals and even expert witness fees to be ordered paid by the other side.

In some private lawsuits, lawyers will usually take the case on a percentage of the potential judgment (usually 1/3 but can be up to 40%). If there is no judgment, then no fees will be due. Note that you will still be responsible to pay for the expenses of filing the documents, photocopying, telephone charges, postage, transcript, reporter and service type fees.

However your fee is arranged, make sure that you have it in writing so that there will be no confusion as to what is owed and when and how it should be paid.

WORKING WITH THE LAWYER

Once you decide to hire the lawyer and the lawyer agrees to take the case, be sure to let the lawyer know what kind of client you are. How involved do you want to be in the case? Do you want to be informed of each step in the case? Would you like copies of each document the lawyer files or receives in your case? Realize that you may be expected to pay for copies if there are costs involved. Alternatively, you may ask you lawyer to make the file available to you on a regular basis to view at his or her office to keep current with developments in your case.

Your lawyer should be able to take you through the case step-by-step to explain the procedures and anticipated timeline in your case. Ask the lawyer how often you can expect him or her to notify you about your case. If you know the general time line of your case, it will help you understand how often to expect contact from the lawyer. For example, depending on the theory of your case, your lawyer may file a complaint with the federal or state fair employment agency before commencing a lawsuit in court. Once your "right to sue" letter is received your complaint is then able to be filed with the court. This process can take several months. Set up a method of contact that is convenient for you and reasonable for your lawyer.

GLOSSARY

a

assault. To threaten another with force or threat of force. An assault is both a crime and a civil wrong, so the victim who is assaulted can sue for damages.

assault and battery. Often in a civil complaint an assault (threat) is joined with the actual harm threatened (battery).

attorney-client privilege. The legal right of an attorney to keep nearly all client information confidential.

b

back pay. The payment of past wages or benefits lost due to sexual harassment.

battery. An intentional or unlawful touching of the victim. Like the tort of assault, a battery is both a crime and a civil wrong, so the victim can sue for damages. Often a civil complaint which charges a battery will also include an assault (threat) charge.

c

civil lawsuit. A lawsuit filed as a result of a violation of a civil right (such as sexual harassment) created by common law or statute.

complainant. The person who files the complaint.

complaint. The pleading document by which a civil lawsuit is begun.

corroborate. To supplement, or add to, the testimony or information of another person or evidence.

d

damages. The money portion of remedies available to compensate the losses of the sexual harassment victim. Damages can be ordered by a court or agreed upon through a settlement. See also remedies and punitive damages.

defamation. A claim in a civil lawsuit that is based on the harm to one's reputation. Slander is the spoken form of libel which is written.

defendant. A person, employer, school or other party who is sued.

e

EEOC. The abbreviation used for the federal Equal Employment Opportunity Commission which is the agency charged with enforcing laws against sexual harassment in the workplace.

EEOC guidelines. The interpretation of the Civil Rights laws that the EEOC will use to enforce the sexual harassment laws.

employee. A person who is hired to perform work for another person, company or school.

employer. A person, company or school who hires a person to perform work.

evidence. Proof which supports a party's case.

f

FEPA. A state's fair employment agency is often called an FEPA.

front pay. The payment of future wages or benefits lost due to sexual harassment.

g

general civility code. A set of social rules in which people treat others with respect.

h

hostile hallways study. The first scientific study of teenagers on sexual harassment in schools.

hostile work environment. Sometimes called "hostile environment." This is a type of sexual harassment claim in which the plaintiff cannot demonstrate that she was fired, but the environment has so much harassing conduct that it will still be considered sexual harassment.

i

injunction. A court order which either prohibits or compels the performance of a particular action. For example, a court may order a company to develop a sexual harassment policy or to hold a training. Or an injunction can order a company to cease sexually harassing activity.

intentional infliction of emotional distress. A type of claim in a civil lawsuit that states that an employee suffered emotional distress from an employer's outrageous conduct. This claim is sometimes called the tort of "outrage."

l

love contract. Not really contracts at all, these are methods used by employers to avoid their responsibility for addressing sexual harassment.

m

mediation. A process by which a claim can be resolved without going to trial.

mitigation of damages. The duty of a sexual harassment victim to reduce loss. For example, if a person loses her job due to sexual harassment, she has a duty to use reasonable efforts to seek other comparable employment.

o

OCR. The Office for Civil Rights (OCR) of the Department of Education is the agency which enforces law prohibiting sexual harassment in federally funded schools.

p

pain and suffering. A part of a claim for money damages which is based on the plaintiff's mental and emotional distress.

plaintiff. A person who files a civil lawsuit.

punitive damages. The money awarded to punish a company, school or other sexual harasser that has engaged in willful or malicious conduct. In some jurisdictions, this is also called "exemplary damages."

q

quid pro quo. A Latin phrase that means "something for something." It is one of the types of sexual harassment claims in which a supervisor, for example, conditions a raise on submission to sex.

r

reasonable person standard. The measure by which a person's actions will be judged as reasonable. The reasonable person will be presumed to exercise due care and ordinary judgment in responding to a situation. In this way, the law can establish a basis by which to measure the reasonableness of conduct.

remedies. The methods by which a person who is victimized by sexual harassment can recover her or his losses. The law permits back pay, reinstatement, future earnings and money damages due to pain and suffering in sexual harassment cases.

retaliation. Acts of a company or school designed to get revenge for a complaint of sexual harassment or to punish a student or employee for the student or employee's cooperation in an investigation of sexual harassment.

right-to-sue letter. The letter issued by the EEOC that gives a worker permission to file a discrimination lawsuit against an employer in federal court.

S

sex discrimination. The illegal and unfair treatment of an employee or student because of that employee's sex.

sexual harassment. Unwanted sexual conduct or words in the workplace or at school which can be the basis of a civil rights complaint. There are two types: quid pro quo and hostile work environment.

sexual harassment policy. The process and procedures a company or school uses to make decisions about how it will respond to sexual harassment.

sexual stereotyping. Judging a person with preconceived notions of gender. For example, the view that women are not tough enough to be police officers.

strict liability. A policy that imposes responsibility on an employer for sexual harassment because the harasser is a supervisor.

t

Title IX. The portion of the Education Code that prohibits sexual harassment in federally funded schools.

Title VII. The portion of the Civil Rights Act of federal law that prohibits sexual harassment in the workplace by employers with 15 or more employees.

tort. A private or civil wrong that causes injury to a person.

u

unwelcome conduct. Behavior or conduct with is not consented to by the person it is targeted at. This must be shown in sexual harassment cases (except where the victim is a child).

APPENDIX A

EEOC OFFICES

Information about the EEOC and the laws it enforces can be found at the following Internet address:
http://www.eeoc.gov.

HEADQUARTERS
U.S. Equal Employment Opportunity Commission
1801 L Street, N.W.
Washington, D.C. 20507
Ph.: (202) 663-4900;
TTY: (202) 663-4494

FIELD OFFICES
To be automatically connected with the nearest EEOC field office, call:
Ph: 1-800-669-4000;
TTY: 1-800-669-6820.

ALBUQUERQUE DISTRICT OFFICE
505 Marquette Street, N.W., Suite 900
Albuquerque, NM 87102
Ph: 505-248-5201
TTY: 505-248-5240

ATLANTA DISTRICT OFFICE

100 Alabama Street, Suite 4R30
Atlanta, GA 30303
Ph: 404-562-6800
TTY: 404-562-6801

BALTIMORE DISTRICT OFFICE

City Crescent Building,
10 South Howard Street, 3rd Floor
Baltimore, MD 21201
Ph: 410-962-3932
TTY: 410-962-6065

BIRMINGHAM DISTRICT OFFICE

Ridge Park Place
1130 22nd Street, Suite 2000
Birmingham, AL 32205
Ph: 205-731-0082
TTY: 205-731-0095

BOSTON AREA OFFICE

1 Congress Street
10th Floor, Room 1001
Boston, MA 02114
Ph: 617-565-3200
TTY: 617-565-3204

BUFFALO LOCAL OFFICE

6 Fountain Plaza, Suite 350
Buffalo, NY 14202
Ph: 716-551-4441
TTY: 716-551-5923

CHARLOTTE DISTRICT OFFICE
129 West Trade Street, Suite 400
Charlotte, NC 28202
Ph: 704-344-6682
TTY: 704-344-6684

CHICAGO DISTRICT OFFICE
500 West Madison Street, Suite 2800
Chicago, IL 60661
Ph: 312-353-2713
TTY: 312-353-2421

CINCINNATI AREA OFFICE
525 Vine Street, Suite 810
Cincinnati, OH 45202-3122
Ph: 513-684-2851
TTY: 513-684-2074

CLEVELAND DISTRICT OFFICE
1660 West Second Street, Suite 850
Cleveland, OH 44113-1454
Ph: 216-522-2001
TTY: 216-522-8441

DALLAS DISTRICT OFFICE
207 S. Houston Street, 3rd Floor
Dallas, TX 75202-4726
Phone: 214-655-3355
TTY: 214-655-3363

DENVER DISTRICT OFFICE
303 E. 17th Avenue, Suite 510
Denver, CO 80203
Ph: 303-866-1300
TTY: 303-866-1950

DETROIT DISTRICT OFFICE
477 Michigan Avenue, Room 865
Detroit, MI 48226-9704
Ph: 313-226-7636
TTY: 313-226-7599

EL PASO AREA OFFICE
The Commons
Building C, Suite 100
4171 N. Mesa Street
El Paso, TX 79902
Ph: 915-832-6550
TTY: 915-832-6545

FRESNO LOCAL OFFICE
1265 West Shaw Avenue, Suite 103
Fresno, CA 93711
Ph: 559-487-5793
TTY: 559-487-5837

GREENSBORO LOCAL OFFICE
801 Summit Avenue
Greensboro, NC 27405-7813
Ph: 336-333-5174
TTY: 336-333-5542

GREENVILLE LOCAL OFFICE
Wachovia Building, Suite 530
15 South Main Street
Greenville, SC 29601
Ph: 864-241-4400
TTY: 864-241-4403

HONOLULU LOCAL OFFICE

300 Ala Moana Boulevard
Room 7123-A
P.O. Box 50082
Honolulu, HI 96850-0051
Ph: 808-541-3120
TTY: 808-541-3131

HOUSTON DISTRICT OFFICE

1919 Smith Street, 7th Floor
Houston, TX 77002
Ph: 713-209-3320
TTY: 713-209-3367

INDIANAPOLIS DISTRICT OFFICE

101 W. Ohio Street, Suite 1900
Indiana, IN 46204-4203
Ph: 317-226-7212
TTY: 317-226-5162

JACKSON AREA OFFICE

Dr. A.H. McCoy Federal Building
100 West Capitol Street, Suite 207
Jackson, MS 39269
Ph: 601-965-4537
TTY: 601-965-4915

KANSAS CITY AREA OFFICE

400 State Avenue, Suite 905
Kansas City, KS 66101
Ph: 913-551-5655
TTY: 913-551-5657

LITTLE ROCK AREA OFFICE
425 West Capitol Avenue, Suite 625
Little Rock, AR 72201
Ph: 501-324-5060
TTY: 501-324-5481

LOS ANGELES DISTRICT OFFICE
255 E. Temple, 4th Floor
Los Angeles, CA 90012
Ph: 213-894-1000
TTY: 213-894-1121

LOUISVILLE AREA OFFICE
600 Dr. Martin Luther King Jr. Place, Suite 268,
Louisville, KY 40202
Ph: 502-582-6082
TTY: 502-582-6285

MEMPHIS DISTRICT OFFICE
1407 Union Avenue, Suite 521
Memphis, TN 38104
Ph: 901-544-0115
TTY: 901-544-0112

MIAMI DISTRICT OFFICE
One Biscayne Tower
2 South Biscayne Boulevard, Suite 2700
Miami, FL 33131
Ph: 305-536-4491
TTY: 305-536-5721

MILWAUKEE DISTRICT OFFICE
310 West Wisconsin Avenue, Suite 800
Milwaukee, WI 53203-2292
Ph: 414-297-1111
TTY: 414-297-1115

MINNEAPOLIS AREA OFFICE

330 South Second Avenue, Suite 430
Minneapolis, MN 55401-2224
Ph: 612-335-4040
TTY: 612-335-4045

NASHVILLE AREA OFFICE

50 Vantage Way, Suite 202
Nashville, TN 37228
Ph: 615-736-5820
TTY: 615-736-5870

NEWARK AREA OFFICE

1 Newark Center, 21st Floor
Newark, NJ 07102-5233
Ph: 973-645-6383
TTY: 973-645-3004

NEW ORLEANS DISTRICT OFFICE

701 Loyola Avenue, Suite 600
New Orleans, LA 70113-9936
Ph: 504-589-2329
TTY: 504-589-2958

NEW YORK DISTRICT OFFICE

201 Varick Street, Suite 1009
New York, NY 10014
Ph: 212-741-2783
TTY: 212-741-3080

NORFOLK AREA OFFICE

Federal Building, Suite 739
200 Granby Street
Norfolk, VA 23510
Ph: 757-441-3470
TTY: 757-441-3578

OAKLAND LOCAL OFFICE
1301 Clay Street, Suite 1170-N
Oakland, CA 94612-5217
Ph: 510-637-3230
TTY: 510-637-3234

OKLAHOMA AREA OFFICE
210 Park Avenue
Oklahoma City, OK 73102
Ph: 405-231-4911
TTY: 405-231-5745

PHILADELPHIA DISTRICT OFFICE
21 South 5th Street, 4th Floor
Philadephia, PA 19106
Ph: 215-440-2600
TTY: 215-440-2610

PHOENIX DISTRICT OFFICE
3300 N. Central Avenue, Suite 690
Phoenix, AZ 85012-1848
Ph: 602-640-5000
TTY: 602-640-5072

PITTSBURGH AREA OFFICE
1001 Liberty Avenue, Suite 300
Pittsburgh, PA 15222-4187
Ph: 412-644-3444
TTY: 412-644-2720

RALEIGH AREA OFFICE
1309 Annapolis Drive
Raleigh, NC 27608-2129
Ph: 919-856-4064
TTY: 919-856-4296

RICHMOND AREA OFFICE
3600 West Broad Street, Room 229
Richmond, VA 23230
Ph: 804-278-4651
TTY: 804-278-4654

SAN ANTONIO DISTRICT OFFICE
5410 Fredericksburg Road, Suite 200
San Antonio, TX 78229-3555
Ph: 210-281-7600
TTY: 210-281-7610

SAN DIEGO AREA OFFICE
401 B Street, Suite 1550
San Diego, CA 92101
Ph: 619-557-7235
TTY: 619-557-7232

SAN FRANCISCO DISTRICT OFFICE
901 Market Street, Suite 500
San Francisco, CA 94103
Phone: 415-356-5100
TTY: 415-356-5098

SAN JOSE LOCAL OFFICE
96 North 3rd Street, Suite 200
San Jose, CA 95112
Ph: 408-291-7352
TTY: 408-291-7374

SAVANNAH LOCAL OFFICE
410 Mall Boulevard, Suite G
Savannah, GA 31406-4821
Ph: 912-652-4234
TTY: 912-652-4439

SEATTLE DISTRICT OFFICE
Federal Office Building
909 First Avenue, Suite 400
Seattle, WA 98104-1061
Ph: 206-220-6883
TTY: 206-220-6882

ST. LOUIS DISTRICT OFFICE
Robert A. Young Building
1222 Spruce Street, Room 8.100
St. Louis, MO 63103
Phone: 314-539-7800
TTY: 314-539-7803

TAMPA AREA OFFICE
501 East Polk Street
10th Floor
Tampa, FL 33602
Ph: 813-228-2310
TTY: 813-228-2003

WASHINGTON FIELD OFFICE
1400 L Street, N.W. Suite 200
Washington, D.C. 20005
Ph: 202-275-7377
TTY: 202-275-7518

APPENDIX B

UNITED STATES DEPARTMENT OF EDUCATION, OFFICE FOR CIVIL RIGHTS— NATIONAL AND REGIONAL OFFICES

NATIONAL OFFICE

US Department of Education
Office for Civil Rights
Mary E. Swtzer Building
330 C St.,SW
Washington, DC, 20202

REGION I: CONNECTICUT, MAINE, MASSACHUSETTS, NEW HAMPSHIRE, RHODE ISLAND, VERMONT

Regional Civil Rights Director
U.S. Department of Education
Office for Civil Rights, Region I
John W. McCormack POCH
Post Office Square, Room 222
Boston, Massachusetts, 02109
Ph: 617-223-9662
TTD: 617- 223-9664

REGION II: NEW JERSEY, NEW YORK, PUERTO RICO, VIRGIN ISLANDS

Regional Civil Rights Director
U.S. Department of Education
Office for Civil Rights, Region II
75 Park Place, 14th Floor,
New York, NY 10007
Ph: 718-488-3550
TTD: 212-264-9464

REGIONAL III: DELAWARE, DISTRICT OF COLUMBIA, MARYLAND, PENNSYLVANIA, VIRGINIA, WEST VIRGINIA

Regional Civil Rights Director
U.S. Department of Education
Office for Civil Rights, Region III
Gateway Building
3535 Market Street
Post Office Box 13716
Philadelphia, PA 19104
Ph: 215-596-6772
TTD: 215-596-6794

REGION IV: ALABAMA, FLORIDA, GEORGIA, KENTUCKY, MISSISSIPPI, NORTH CAROLINA, SOUTH CAROLINA, TENNESSEE

Regional Civil Rights Director
U.S. Department of Education
Office for Civil Rights, Region IV
101 Marietta Tower—27th Floor
P. O. Box 1705
Atlanta, Georgia 30301
Ph: 404-331-2954
TTD: 404-331-2010

REGION V: ILLINOIS, INDIANA, MINNESOTA, MICHIGAN, OHIO, WISCONSIN

Regional Civil Rights Director
U.S. Department of Education
Office for Civil Rights, Region V
401 South State Street—7th Fl.
Chicago, Illinois 60605
Ph: 312-353-3520
TTD: 312-353-2540

REGION VI: ARKANSAS, LOUISIANA, NEW MEXICO, OKLAHOMA, TEXAS

Regional Civil Rights Director
U.S. Department of Education
Office for Civil Rights, Region VI
1200 Main Tower Building—Suite 2260
Dallas, Texas 75202
Ph: 214-767-3936
TTD: 214-767-3315

REGION VII: IOWA, KANSAS, MISSOURI, NEBRASKA

Regional Civil Rights Director
U.S. Department of Education
Office for Civil Rights, Region VII
P. O. Box 901381
10220 N. Executive Hills Blvd., 8th Fl.
Kansas City, Missouri 64190-1381
Ph: 816-891-8026
TTD: 816-374-7607

REGION VIII: COLORADO, MONTANA, NORTH DAKOTA, SOUTH DAKOTA, UTAH, WYOMING

Regional Civil Rights Director
U.S. Department of Education
Office for Civil Rights, Region VIII
1961 Stout Street, Room 342
Denver, Colorado 80294
Ph: 303-844-5695
TTD: 303-844-3417

REGION IX: ARIZONA, CALIFORNIA, HAWAII, NEVADA, GUAM, TRUST TERRITORIES OF THE PACIFIC ISLANDS, AMERICAN SAMOA

Regional Civil Rights Director
U.S. Department of Education
Office for Civil Rights, Region IX
221 Main Street, 10th Floor
San Francisco, CA 94105
Ph: 415-227-8020
TTD: 415-227-8124

REGION X: ALASKA, IDAHO, OREGON, WASHINGTON

Regional Civil Rights Director
U.S. Department of Education
Office for Civil Rights, Region X
2901 3rd Avenue—Room 100
Seattle, Washington 98121-1042
Ph: 206-442-1635
TTD: 206-442-4542

APPENDIX C

TITLE VII OF THE CIVIL RIGHTS ACT

Law: 42 U.S.C. Sec. 2000e.

Scope: Employers with at least fifteen employees who work at least twenty weeks a year, but excludes bona fide nonprofit private membership clubs.

Covers: Among other things, Title VII prohibits employment discrimination based sex. It is an unlawful employment practice for an employer (1) to fail or refuse to hire or to discharge or otherwise to discriminate against any individual with respect to his compensation, terms, conditions, or privileges of employment, because of such individual's sex; or (2) to limit, segregate, or classify employees or applicants for employment that deprives them of employment opportunities or otherwise adversely affects their status as employees, because of sex. It is also unlawful for an employment agency to fail or refuse to refer for employment, or otherwise to discriminate against, any individual because of sex or refer for employment any individual on the basis of his sex. Also prohibited is sex discrimination in apprenticeship or other training or retraining, including on –the –job training programs. However, there is an exception where sex is a bona fide occupational qualification that is reasonably necessary to the normal operation of the particular business.

Retaliation for filing a charge or cooperating in the investigation of a charge is also prohibited.

Remedies: Hiring, reinstatement, promotion, back pay, temporary restraining orders, attorneys fees, and other appropriate relief.

Agency: Equal Employment Opportunity Commission (EEOC)
1-800-669-4000 (voice)
1-800-669-6820 (TTY) to contact the nearest EEOC office for the office closest to you.

APPENDIX D

TITLE IX OF THE EDUCATIONAL CODE

Law: 42 U.S.C. Sec. 1988, 20 U.S.C. Sec. 1682.

Scope: Federally funded schools.

Covers: Among other things, Title IX prohibits discrimination based sex for covered schools. Sexual harassment has been found to be a form of sex discrimination.

Retaliation for filing a charge or cooperating in the investigation of a charge is also prohibited.

Remedies: Money damages and "make whole" remedies are available

Agency: OCR headquarters office in Washington D.C.:
U.S. Department of Education
Office for Civil Rights
Customer Service Team
Mary E. Switzer Building
330 C Street, SW
Washington, D.C. 20202
1-800-421-3481
TDD: 877-521-2172

You may also contact the OCR enforcement office serving your state or territory call 800-421-3481 for the OCR office closest to you.

Website: www.ed.gov/offices/OCR

APPENDIX E

STATE-BY-STATE
FAIR EMPLOYMENT PRACTICES
LAWS AND ANTI-DISCRIMINATION
ENFORCEMENT AGENCIES

ALABAMA

Law: Code of Alabama, Section 29-4-3.

Scope: Applies to employees of the Legislature.

Covers: In the selection of the employees of the Legislature, there shall be no discrimination on account of sex. (Secs. 29-4-3.)

Remedies: None listed.

Agency: Alabama Department of Human Resources
Office of Equal Employment & Civil Rights
50 N. Ripley Street
Montgomery, AL 36130
334-242-1310

Website: http://www.dhr.state.al.us/eeo/

ALASKA

Law: Alaska Statutes, Sections18.80.010 to
             18.80.300.

Scope: Public and private employers, employment
             agencies, labor organizations, communications
             media, but not domestic workers, social clubs
             or not-for-profits. (Secs. 18.80.220, 18.80.300.)

Covers: It is unlawful for an employer to refuse to hire
             or discriminate in compensation, term, condi-
             tion or privilege of employment because of a
             person's sex. (Sec. 18.80.220.)

Remedies: Hiring, reinstatement, promotion, back pay,
             temporary restraining orders, attorneys fees,
             other appropriate relief.

Agency: Office of Equal Employment Opportunity
             550 West 7th Avenue, Suite 1010
             Anchorage, Alaska 99501
             1-800-797-7495

Website: http://www.eeo.state.ak.us/eeo/eeomission.html

ARIZONA

Law: Arizona Revised Statutes Annotated, Sections
            41-1461 to 1466, 41-1481 to 1485.

Scope: State and private employers, employment agen-
            cies, labor organizations, but not employers
            with less than fifteen workers, certain staff of
            elected officials or private nonprofit member-
            ship clubs. (Secs. 41-1461.)

Covers: It is unlawful for an employer to fail or refuse
            to hire or to discharge or otherwise discrimi-
            nate against any individual regarding compen-
            sation, terms, conditions or privileges of
            employment on the basis of sex. (Sec. 41-1463.)

Remedies: Hiring, reinstatement, promotion, back pay,
            temporary restraining orders, attorneys fees to
            prevailing party, other appropriate relief.

Agency: Arizona Civil Rights Division
            1275 West Washington
            Phoenix, Arizona 85007
            602-542-5263
            TDD: 602-542-5002

Website: http://www.state.az.us/

ARKANSAS

Law: Arkansas Code Annotated.

Scope: Applies to state employees. (Sec. 21-12-103.)

Covers: Every state agency shall include in its personnel manual a statement that discrimination by any officer or employee based upon sex shall constitute grounds for dismissal. When it is determined by any court of law that any employee of this state is guilty of discrimination based upon sex, it is grounds for dismissal from employment. (Sec. 1-12-103 (a),(b).)

Remedies: None listed.

CALIFORNIA

Law: West's Annotated California codes, Government Code. Fair Employment Practices and Housing Act, Sections 12900 to 12996.

Scope: Public and private employers, employment agencies, labor organizations employing five or more employees, but not certain family members or nonprofit religious organizations. (Sec. 12926, 12940.)

Covers: The opportunity to seek and obtain and hold employment without discrimination because of sex is a civil right. (Sec.12921.) It is an unlawful employment practice, unless based on a bona fide occupational qualification or applicable security regulations, for an employer, because of sex, to refuse to hire or employ the person or to refuse to select the person for a training program leading to employment or to bar or discharge any the person from employment or from a training program leading to employment or to discriminate against the person in compensation or in terms, conditions or privileges of employment. (Sec. 12940.) Requires the employer to ensure a workplace free of sexual harassment by posting information on the illegality of sexual harassment and retaliation and providing information individually to employees listing descriptions of sexually harassing conduct and the employer's internal complaint process as well as methods

(continued)

for filing a complaint with the state's fair employment practice agency. (Sec. 12950.)

Remedies: Hiring, reinstatement, promotion, back pay, temporary restraining orders, cease and desist orders, attorneys fees, other appropriate relief such as monetary damages.

Agency: California Department of Fair Employment and Housing
2000 O Street Ste. 120
Sacramento, CA 95814-5212

Website: http://www.dfeh.ca.gov/

COLORADO

Law: West's Colorado Revised Statutes Annotated, Sections 24-34-301 to -406.

Scope: Public and private employers, employment agencies, labor organizations, but not domestic workers or tax exempt religious organizations. (Secs. 4-34-401.)

Covers: It is a discriminatory employment practice for an employer to refuse to hire, discharge, promote or demote, to harass or to discriminate in compensation against any qualified person on the basis of sex. To harass includes to create a hostile work environment based on a person's sex. (Sec. 24-34-402.)

Remedies: Hiring, reinstatement, promotion, back pay, cease and desist order.

Agency: Colorado Civil Rights Division Central Office
1560 Broadway, Room #1050
Denver, CO 80202-5143
800-262-4845
TDD: 303-894-7880

Website: http://www.dora.state.co.us/civil-rights/

CONNECTICUT

Law: Connecticut General Statutes Annotated, Sections 46a-51 to -99. Fair Employment Practices Act.

Scope: Public and private employers, employment agencies, labor organizations, but not employers of less than three workers, domestic or family workers. (Sec. 46a-51.)

Covers: It is a discriminatory practice for an employer or his agent to refuse to hire or to bar or fire any person or to discriminate in compensation, terms, conditions or privileges of employment because of sex or to sexually harass an applicant or an employee. (Sec. 46a-60.)

Remedies: Hiring, reinstatement, promotion, back pay (less interim earnings), temporary restraining orders (applies to employers of fifty or more), cease and desist orders and other appropriate relief.

Agency: Connecticut Commission on Human Rights and Opportunities
1229 Albany Avenue
Hartford, CT 06112-2193
Ph. (860) 566-7710;
TDD: (860) 566-7710

Website: http://www.state.ct.us/chro/

DELAWARE

Law: Delaware Code Annotated, Title 19, Sections
            710-718.

Scope: Public and private employers, employment
            agencies, labor organizations, but not employers
            of less than four workers, domestic, agricultural
            or family workers or private charitable organi-
            zations. (Secs. 710, 711.)

Covers: It shall be an unlawful employment practice for
            an employer to fail or refuse to hire or to dis-
            charge any person or otherwise discriminate on
            the basis of compensation, terms, conditions or
            privileges of employment because of sex.
            (Sec. 711.)

Remedies: Hiring, reinstatement, promotion, back pay
            (less interim earnings), cease and desist order,
            attorneys fees to prevailing party and other
            appropriate relief.

Agency: Delaware Dept. of Labor,
            Division of Industrial Affairs
            4425 N. Market Street
            Wilmington, Delaware 19802
            302-761-8200

Website: http://www.state.de.us/

DISTRICT OF COLUMBIA

Law: District of Columbia Code Ann.
               Sections 2-1401.01 to -2-1403.17.

Scope: Government and private employers, employ-
               ment agencies, labor organizations, but not
               domestic or family workers. (Sec. 2-1401.02.)

Covers: It is an unlawful discriminatory practice to fail
               or refuse to hire, or to discharge any individual
               or to otherwise discriminate against any person
               because of compensation, terms, conditions or
               privileges of employment including promotion,
               deprivation of employment opportunities or
               adverse affect on an individual's employment
               status on the basis of sex. (Sec. 2-1402.11.)

Remedies: Hiring, reinstatement, promotion, back pay,
               temporary restraining orders, cease and desist
               order, money damages, attorneys fees, other
               appropriate relief.

Agency: District of Columbia Commission on
               Human Rights
               441 4th Street, NW, Ste. 970 N.
               Wash. D.C. 20001
               202-724-1385

FLORIDA

Law: Florida Statutes Annotated,
Sections 760.01 to 760.11.

Scope: Public and private employers, employment
agencies, labor organizations, employers with
less than fifteen workers. (Secs. 60.02, 760.10.)

Covers: It is an unlawful employment practice for an
employer to discharge, or fail or refuse to hire
any person or otherwise discriminate against
any individual with respect to compensation,
terms, conditions, or privileges of employment
because of sex. It is also unlawful to deprive
applicants or employees of employment opportunities or to adversely affect employee status.
(Sec. 760.10.)

Remedies: Appropriate affirmative action, back pay, cease
and desist orders, attorneys fees.

Agency: Florida Commission on Human Relations
325 John Knox Road, Building F, Suite 240
Tallahassee, Florida 32303-4149
800-342-8170
TDD ASCII 800-955-1339
Baudot 800-955-8771

Website: http://fchr.state.fl.us/

GEORGIA

Law: Official Code of Georgia Annotated, Sections 45-19-20 to 45-19-45.

Scope: Public employers which employ at least fifteen workers or staff of public officials. (Secs. 45-19-22.)

Covers: It is an unlawful employment practice for an employer to fail or refuse to hire, to discharge, or otherwise to discriminate against any person regarding compensation, term, conditions, privileges of employment because of sex. It is also unlawful to segregate or classify employees to deprive employment opportunities or otherwise adversely affect employment status. (Sec. 45-19-29.)

Remedies: Hiring, reinstatement, promotion, back pay (less interim earnings), cease and desist orders, actual money damages, attorneys fees to prevailing party if case goes to court, other appropriate relief.

Agency: Georgia Commission on Equal Opportunity 710 Cain Towers, Peachtree Center, 229 Peachtree Street, NW Atlanta, GA 30303 800-362-0951

Website: http://www.dhr.state.ga.us/Departments/DHR/

HAWAII

Law: Hawaii Revised Statutes, Sections 378-1 to -38. Hawaii Fair Employment Practices Act.

Scope: Public and private employers, employment agencies, labor organizations, but not domestic workers. (Sec. 378-1.)

Covers: It is an unlawful discriminatory practice where because of sex an employer refuses to hire, employ or bars or discharges an employee or otherwise discriminates in compensation, terms, conditions or privileges of employment. It is also unlawful for any person to aid, abet, incite, compel or coerce the doing of any discriminatory practice. (Sec. 378-1.)

Remedies: Hiring, reinstatement, back pay, injunctions, cease and desist orders, attorneys fees to prevailing plaintiffs, other appropriate relief. **NOTE:** *Where judgment is not paid within thirty days, court can order a respondent to close business until judgment is paid.*

Agency: Hawaii Civil Rights Commission
830 Punchbowl Street, Room 411
Honolulu, HI 96813
808-586-8636

Website: http://www.state.hi.us/hcrc/

IDAHO

Law: Idaho Code Ann. Sections 67-5901 to 67-5911.

Scope: Public and private employers, employment agencies, labor organizations, but not employers with less than five workers. (Secs. 67-5902, 67-5908.)

Covers: It is prohibited to discriminate against a person because of sex. It is prohibited for an employer to fire or refuse to hire, to discharge, or to otherwise discriminate against a person with respect to compensation, terms, conditions, privileges of employment or to reduce the wage or an employee to comply with the law. It is also prohibited to classify or segregate so as to limit employment opportunities or to adversely affect status of an employee or to cause or attempt to cause an employer to violate the anti-discrimination law. (Sec. 67-5909.)

Remedies: Hiring, reinstatement, promotion, back pay, cease and desist orders, actual damages, other appropriate relief.

Agency: Idaho Human Rights Commission
              1109 Main Street, Ste 400
              P. O. Box 83720
              Boise, ID 83720-0040
              888-249-7025
              TTY 208-334-4751

Website: http://www.state.id.us/ihrc/

ILLINOIS

Law: West's Illinois Compiled Statutes Annotated.
           775 ILCS 5/1-101 to 5/10-102 Illinois Human
           Rights Act; also ILCS Const. Art. I, Section 18.

Scope: Public and private employers, employment
           agencies, labor organizations, but not domestic
           or certain vocational workers, religious organi-
           zations, public officials and staffs.
           (Secs. 5/2-101.)

Covers: It is a civil rights violation for any employer to
           refuse to hire, to segregate, or to act with
           respect to recruitment, hiring, promotion,
           renewal of employment, selection for training
           or apprenticeship, discharge, discipline, tenure
           or terms, privileges or conditions of employ-
           ment on the basis of sex. Sexual harassment
           means any unwelcome sexual advances or
           requests for sexual favors or any conduct of a
           sexual nature when (1) submission to such
           conduct is made either explicitly or implicitly a
           term or condition of an individual's employ-
           ment, (2) submission to or rejection of such
           conduct by an individual is used as the basis for
           employment decisions affecting such individ-
           ual, or (3) such conduct has the purpose or
           effect of substantially interfering with an indi-
           vidual's work performance or creating an
           intimidating, hostile or offensive working envi-
           ronment. (Sec. 5/2-101, 5/2-102.)

(continued)

Remedies: Hiring, reinstatement, promotion, back pay, temporary restraining and cease and desist orders, actual damages, attorneys fees, other appropriate relief.

Agency: Illinois Department of Human Rights
100 West Randolph, Ste 10-100
Chicago, Illinois 60601
312-814-6200.

Website: http://www.state.il.us/dhr/

INDIANA

Law: Burns Ind. Code Annotated,
              Sections 22-9-1-2 to 22-9-1-13.

Scope: Public and private employers, employment
              agencies, labor organizations, but not employers
              with less than six workers, domestic or certain
              family workers, social, nonprofit, or religious
              organizations. (Secs. 22-9-1-3.)

Covers: It is the policy of this state to provide all citi-
              zens with equal opportunities for employment.
              (Sec. 22-9-1-2.) The exclusion of a person from
              equal opportunities because of sex is an unlawful
              discriminatory practice unless based on a bona
              fide occupational qualification which is
              reasonably necessary to the normal operation
              of the business. (Sec. 22-9-1-3.)

Remedies: Affirmative action, including back pay, cease
              and desist orders, other appropriate relief.

Agency: The Indiana Civil Rights Commission,
              Indiana Government Center North
              100 North Senate Avenue, Room N103
              Indianapolis, IN 46204
              800-628-2909
              TTY 800-743-3333

Website: http://www.state.in.us/icrc/

IOWA

Law: Iowa Code Annotated, Section 216.
Iowa Civil Rights Act.

Scope: Public and private employers, employment
agencies, labor organizations, but not employers
with less than four workers, domestic or certain
family workers. (Secs. 216.2, 216.6.)

Covers: It is an unfair or discriminatory practice for any
person to refuse to hire, accept, register, classify
or refer for employment, to discharge any
employee, or to otherwise discriminate in
employment against any applicant because of
sex, unless based on the nature of the
occupation.

Remedies: Hiring, reinstatement, promotion, back pay
(less interim earnings), actual damages,
attorneys' fees, other appropriate relief.

Agency: Iowa Department of Human Rights
Lucas State Office Building
Des Moines, Iowa 50319
515-281-7300

Website: http://www.state.ia.us/government/dhr/

KANSAS

Law:　　Kansas Statutes Annotated, Sections 44-1001 to-1311. Kansas Act Against Discrimination.

Scope:　　Public and private employers, employment agencies, labor and social service organizations, but not employers with less than four workers, domestic or certain family workers, or social or nonprofit organizations. (Secs. 44-1002.)

Covers:　　It is an unlawful employment practice for an employer, because of sex, to refuse to hire or employ such person to bar or discharge such person from employment or to otherwise discriminate against such person in compensation, terms, conditions or privileges of employment; to limit segregate, separate, classify or make any distinction in regards to employees; or to follow any employment procedure or practice which results in discrimination without a valid business necessity. (Sec. 44-1009.)

Remedies:　　Hiring, reinstatement, promotion, back pay, cease and desist orders, certain pain and suffering damages and actual damages, other appropriate relief.

(continued)

Agency: Kansas Human Rights Commission
900 SW Jackson, Suite 851
South Landon Office Building
Topeka, KS 66612-1258
785-296-3206
TTY 785-296-0245

Website: http://www.ink.org/public/khrc/

KENTUCKY

Law: Kentucky Revised Statutes Annotated,
            Sections 344.010-500, 344.207.170.
            Chapter 344. Civil Rights.

Scope: Employers, employment agencies, labor organi-
            zations, but not employers with less than eight
            workers, domestic or certain family workers.
            (Secs. 344.020, 344.010-.070.)

Covers: It is an unlawful practice for an employer to
            fail or refuse to hire, or to discharge any indi-
            vidual, or otherwise to discriminate against an
            individual with respect to compensation, terms,
            conditions, or privileges of employment
            because of the individual's sex. (Sec. 344.040.)

Remedies: Hiring, reinstatement, promotion, back pay
            (less interim earnings), temporary restraining
            and cease and desist orders, damages, attorneys
            fees, other appropriate relief.

Agency: Kentucky Commission on Human Rights
            Suite 700, The Heyburn Building
            332 W. Broadway
            Louisville, KY 40202
            800-292-5566
            TDD 502-595-4084

Website: http://www.state.ky.us/agencies2/kchr/

LOUISIANA

Law: West's Louisiana Statutes Annotated,
             Section 23-301-340. Louisiana Employment
             Discrimination Law.

Scope: Public and private employers, employment
             agencies, labor organizations, but not employers
             with less than twenty workers, religious, or
             nonprofit organizations. (Sec. 23-302.)

Covers: It is unlawful for an employer to intentionally
             fail or refuse to hire, or to discharge any indi-
             vidual, or otherwise intentionally discriminate
             against an individual with respect to his com-
             pensation or his terms, conditions, or privileges
             of employment because of the individual's sex
             unless as a result of a bona fide occupational
             qualification reasonably necessary for the nor-
             mal operation of business. (Sec. 23-332.)

Remedies: Hiring, reinstatement, promotion, back pay,
             damages, attorneys fees, other appropriate
             relief.

Agency: Louisiana Commission on Human Rights
             1001 N. 23rd St., Suite 262
             Baton Rouge, Louisiana 70802
             225-342-6969
             TDD 888-248-0859

Website: http://www.gov.state.la.us/depts/lchr.htm

MAINE

Law: Maine Revised Statutes Annotated, title V, Sections 4551 to 4632. Maine Human Rights Act.

Scope: Public and private employers and their agents, employment agencies, labor organizations, but not certain family workers. (Secs. 4553, 4572.)

Covers: It is unlawful employment discrimination for any employer to fail or refuse to hire or otherwise discriminate against any applicant for employment or to discharge an employee or discriminate with respect to hire, tenure, promotion, transfer, compensation, terms, conditions or privileges of employment or any other matter directly or indirectly related to employment because of sex, unless based on a bona fide occupational qualification. (Sec. 4572.)

Remedies: Reinstatement, back pay, temporary restraining and cease and desist orders, attorneys fees, other appropriate relief.

Agency: Maine Human Rights Commission
51 State House Station
Augusta, ME 04333-0051
207-624-6050
TTY/TTD 207-624-6064

Website: http://www.state.me.us/mhrc/

MARYLAND

Law: Annotated Code of Maryland, art. 49b, Sections 14-18. Fair Employment Practices Act.

Scope: Public and private employers, employment agencies, labor organizations, but not employers with less than fifteen workers, staffs of public officials and membership clubs. (Secs. 15, 16.)

Covers: It is an unlawful employment practice for an employer to fail or refuse to hire or to discharge an individual or otherwise to discriminate against any individual with respect to the individual's compensation, terms, conditions or privileges of employment because of such individual's sex, unless based on a bona fide occupational qualification. (Sec. 16.)

Remedies: Hiring, reinstatement, promotion, back pay, cease and desist orders, other appropriate relief.

Agency: Maryland Commission on Human Relations
20 East Franklin Street
Baltimore, MD 21202-2274
410-333-1700

Website: http://www.mchr.state.md.us/

MASSACHUSETTS

Law: Annotated Laws of Massachusetts, Chapter
151B., Sections1-10. Massachusetts Fair
Employment Practices Law

Scope: Public and private employers and agents,
employment agencies, labor organizations, but
not employers with less than six workers, nonprofit organizations. (Secs. 1, 4.)

Covers: It is an unlawful employment practice for an
employer or an agent of the employer to refuse
to hire or employ or to bar or to discharge
from employment an individual or to discriminate against an individual in compensation,
terms, conditions or privileges of employment
because of the individual's sex, unless based on
a bona fide occupational qualification. It is also
an unlawful employment practice for an
employer, personally or through its agents, to
sexually harass any employee. (Sec. 4.)

NOTE: *Massachusetts has a specific statutory
requirement for employers to adopt a sexual
harassment policy and to provide the policy to
employees. The policy must include descriptions
and examples of what constitutes sexual harassment along with the process for filing internal
complaints.* (Sec. 3A.)

(continued)

Remedies: Hiring, reinstatement, promotion, back pay, cease and desist and temporary restraining orders, attorneys fees to prevailing party, other appropriate relief.

Agency: Massachusetts Commission Against Discrimination
One Ashburton Place, Rm. 601
Boston, Massachusetts 02108
671-727-3990

MICHIGAN

Law: Michigan Compiled Laws Annotated, Sections 37.2101, 37.202. Elliott-Larsen Civil Rights Act.

Scope: Public and private employers, employment agencies, labor organizations, but not certain family workers. (Sec. 37.2202.)

Covers: An employer shall not fail or refuse to hire or recruit, discharge or otherwise discriminate against an individual with respect to employment, compensation, or a term, condition or privilege of employment because of sex. (Sec. 37.202.)

Remedies: Hiring, reinstatement, promotion, back pay, cease and desist orders, damages, attorneys fees, other appropriate relief.

Agency: Michigan Department of Human Rights
State of Michigan Plaza Bldg., 6th Flr.
1200 Sixth Ave.
Detroit, MI 48226
313-256-2663
WATS 800-482-3604
TDD 313-961-1552

Website: http://www.michigan.gov/mdcr

MINNESOTA

Law: Minnesota Statutes Annotated,
            Section 363.01-363.20. Human Rights.

Scope: Public and private employers, employment
            agencies, labor organizations, but not domestic
            and certain family workers.
            (Secs. 363.01, 363.02.)

Covers: It is an unfair employment practice for an
            employer to refuse to hire or to maintain a sys-
            tem of employment which unreasonably
            excludes a person seeking employment or to
            discharge an employee or to discriminate
            against a person with respect to hiring, tenure,
            compensation, terms, upgrading, conditions
            facilities or privileges of employment because
            of such individual's sex, unless based on a bona
            fide occupational qualification. (Sec. 363.03.)
            Sexual harassment includes unwanted sexual
            advances, requests for sexual favors, sexually
            motivated physical contact or other verbal or
            physical conduct or communication of a sexual
            nature when submission to that conduct is
            made a factor in decision making concerning
            that individual's employment or substantially
            interferes with an individual's employment.
            (Sec. 363.01.subd.41.)

(continued)

Remedies: Hiring, reinstatement, promotion, back pay,
cease and desist orders, damages, attorneys fees
to prevailing party, other appropriate relief.

Agency: Commission on Civil Rights Office
City Hall, Room 239
350 South Fifth Street
Minneapolis, MN 55415
612-673-3012
TTY 612-673-2044

Website: http://www.humanrights.state.mn.us/

MISSISSIPPI

Law: Mississippi Code Annotated, Section 25-9-149.

Scope: Applies to employees in state government.

Covers: No person seeking employment in state service or employed in state service shall be discriminated against on the basis of sex.
(Sec. 25-9-149.)

Remedies: None stated.

MISSOURI

Law: Vernon's Annotated Missouri Statutes Sections 213.010-.130 . Missouri Fair Employment Practices Act and Missouri Code of Regulations § 60-3.040(17).

Scope: Public and private employers, employment agencies, labor organizations, but not employers with less than six workers or religious organizations. (Secs. 213.055, 213.010.)

Covers: It is an unlawful employment practice for an employer to fail or refuse to hire or to discharge an individual or otherwise to discriminate against any individual with respect to the individual's compensation, terms, conditions or privileges of employment because of such individual's sex, or to limit or classify employees or applicants to deprive or tend to deprive them of employment opportunities on the basis of sex. Certain exceptions apply based on a bona fide occupational qualification. (Sec. 213.055.)

Remedies: Hiring, reinstatement, promotion, back pay, cease and desist and temporary restraining orders, money damages, attorneys fees for prevailing parties, other appropriate relief.

(continued)

Agency: Missouri Commission on Human Rights
              PO Box 1129
              3315 West Truman Boulevard
              Jefferson City, MO 65102-1129
              573-751-3325

Website: http://www.dolir.state.mo.us/hr

MONTANA

Law: Montana Code Annotated, Sections 49-1-101 to 49-2-601. Montana Human Rights Act.

Scope: Public and private employers, employment agencies, labor organizations, but not certain not-for-profit agencies.
(Secs. 49-2-303 and 308, 49-2-101.)

Covers: It is an unlawful discriminatory practice for an employer to refuse employment to a person, to bar a person from employment, or to discriminate against a person in compensation, or in a term, condition or privilege of employment because of sex, when the reasonable demands of the position do not require a sex distinction.
(Sec. 49-2-303.)

Remedies: Reasonable measures to correct the discrimination and harm caused, cease and desist orders, temporary orders, attorneys fees to prevailing parties under certain circumstances. Does not allow punitive damages.

Agency: Montana Human Rights Bureau Steamboat Block, 616 Helena Avenue, Suite 302
P.O. Box 1728
Helena, MT 59624-1728
800-542-0807

Website: http://erd.dli.state.mt.us/HumanRights/HRhome.htm

NEBRASKA

Law: Revised Statutes of Nebraska, Sections 48-1101
            to 1126. Nebraska Fair Employment Act

Scope: Public and private employers, employment
            agencies, labor organizations, but not employers
            with less than fifteen workers, domestic and
            certain family workers, and tax-exempt private
            membership clubs.
            (Secs. 8-1102, 48-1104, 48-1106.)

Covers: It is an unlawful employment practice for an
            employer to refuse employment to fail or
            refuse to hire, to discharge or to harass any
            individual, or otherwise to discriminate against
            any individual with respect to compensation,
            terms, conditions or privileges of employment
            because of sex, or to limit, solicit or advertise
            or classify employees on the basis of sex when
            to do so would limit or deprive any individual
            of employment opportunities or status as an
            employee. (Sec. 48-1104.)

Remedies: Hiring, reinstatement, promotion, back pay
            (from which interim earnings are deducted),
            cease and desist orders, attorney fees if case
            goes to court, other appropriate relief.

(continued)

Agency: Nebraska Equal Opportunity Commission
Nebraska State Office Building
301 Centennial Mall South, 5th Floor
P.O. Box 94934
Lincoln, NE 68509-4934
800-642-6112

Website: http://www.nol.org/home/NEOC/

NEVADA

Law: Nevada Revised Statutes Annotated, (Sections
              613.310 to 613.430. Nevada Fair Employment
              Practices Act

Scope: Public and private employers, employment
              agencies, labor organizations, but not employers
              with less than fifteen workers, tax-exempt pri-
              vate membership clubs.
              (Secs. 13.330, 613.310.)

Covers: It is an unlawful employment practice for an
              employer to fail or refuse to hire, or to dis-
              charge any person, or otherwise to discriminate
              against any person with respect to his compen-
              sation, terms, conditions, or privileges of
              employment because of sex unless on the basis
              of a bona fide occupational qualification rea-
              sonably necessary to the normal operation of
              that particular business. (Sec. 613.350.)

Remedies: Hiring, reinstatement, back pay, and other
              appropriate remedies, including interest on lost
              wages, cease and desist orders, temporary relief
              orders.

(continued)

Agency: Nevada Equal Rights Commission Reno Office:
2450 Wrondel Way, Suite C
Reno, Nevada 89502
775-688-1288

Las Vegas Office,
1515 E. Tropicana Avenue, Suite-590
Las Vegas, Nevada-89119
702-486-7161

Website: http://www.state.nv.us/detr/nerc/sexharss.htm

NEW HAMPSHIRE

Law: New Hampshire Statutes Annotated Sections 354-A:1 to A:25. New Hampshire Law Against Discrimination

Scope: Public and private employers, employment agencies, labor organizations, but not employers with less than six workers, domestic and certain family workers, social clubs or nonprofit. (Secs.354-A:7, 354-A:2.)

Covers: It is an unlawful discriminatory practice for an employer because of sex to refuse to hire, employ or to bar or to discharge from employment, or to discriminate against an individual in compensation, or in terms, conditions or privileges of employment because of sex, unless the bona fide demands of the position require a sex distinction. (Sec. 354-A:7(I).) Sexual harassment constitutes sex discrimination. Unwelcome sexual advances, requests for sexual favors, and other verbal, non-verbal or physical conduct of a sexual nature constitutes sexual harassment when: (a) submission to such conduct is made either explicitly or implicitly a term or condition of an individual's employment; (b) Submission to or rejection of such conduct by an individual is used as the basis for employment decisions affecting such individual; or (c) Such conduct has the purpose or effect of unreasonably interfering with an individual's work performance or creating an

(continued)

intimidating, hostile, or offensive working environment. (Sec. 354-A:7(V).)

Remedies: Hiring, reinstatement, promotion, back pay (from which interim earnings are deducted), cease and desist orders, compensatory damages, attorney fees, other appropriate relief.

Agency: New Hampshire Commission for Human Rights
2 Chenell Drive
Concord, NH 03301
603-271-2767

Website: http://www.state.nh.us/hrc/

NEW JERSEY

Law: New Jersey Statutes Annotated Sections 10:5-1 to 10:5-42. New Jersey Law Against Discrimination.

Scope: Public and private employers, employment agencies, labor organizations, but not domestic workers. Secs.10:5-5, 10:5-12.)

Covers: It is an unlawful employment practice for an employer, because of sex, to refuse to hire or employ or to bar or to discharge an individual from employment, or to discriminate against an individual in compensation, or in terms, conditions or privileges of employment because of sex, when the reasonable demands of the position do not require a sex distinction. (Sec.10:5-12(a).)

Remedies: Hiring, reinstatement, promotion, cease and desist orders, attorney fees to prevailing parties (to defendant only if case is brought in bad faith), other appropriate relief.

Agency: New Jersey Division on Civil Rights
140 East Front Street
PO Box 090
Trenton, NJ 08625-0090
609-292-4605
TDD 609-292-1785

Website: http://www.state.nj.us/lps/dcr/

NEW MEXICO

Law: New Mexico Statutes Annotated,
Sections 28-1-1 to 28-1-14.
New Mexico Human Rights Act.

Scope: Public and private employers, employment
agencies, labor organizations, but not employers
with less than four workers.
(Secs. 28-1-2, 28-1-7.)

Cover: It is an unlawful discriminatory practice for an
employer to refuse to hire, to discharge, to promote or demote or to discriminate in matters
of compensation, terms, conditions or privileges
of employment because of sex, unless statuto-
rily prohibited or the reasonable demands of
the position require a sex distinction.
(Sec. 28-1-7(a).)

Remedies: Any necessary affirmative action (such as hiring, reinstatement, promotion, back pay, actual
damages), cease and desist and other injunctive
orders, attorney fees, other appropriate relief.

Agency: New Mexico Human Rights Division
1596 Pacheco Street
Aspen Plaza Suite 103
Santa Fe, New Mexico 87505
(800) 566-9471

Website: http://www.dol.state.nm.us/dol_qhrd.html

NEW YORK

Law:　　McKinney's Consolidated Laws of New York Annotated, Executive Law, (Secs. 290-301.) New York Human Rights Law.

Scope:　　Employers, licensing agencies, employment agencies, labor organizations, but not employers with less than four workers, domestic or certain family workers (Secs.292, 296.)

Covers:　　It is an unlawful discriminatory practice for an employer, because of sex, to refuse to hire or employ or to bar or discharge a person from employment, or to discriminate against an individual in compensation, or in terms, conditions or privileges of employment when the reasonable demands of the position do not require a sex distinction. (Sec.296(1).)

Remedies:　　Hiring, reinstatement, promotion, back pay, cease and desist orders, temporary relief, compensatory damages, other appropriate relief.

Agency:　　Office of Sexual Harassment
New York State Division of Human Rights
Office of Sexual Harassment
55 Hanson Place, Suite 347
Brooklyn, New York 11217
718-722-2060

Website:　　http://www.nysdhr.com/

NORTH CAROLINA

Law: North Carolina General Statutes,
                Sections 143-422.1 to 422.3
                North Carolina Equal Employment Practices Act

Scope: Employers, but not employers with less than
                fifteen workers. (Secs. 143-422.2.)

Covers: The public policy of North Carolina is that
                persons have a right to seek employment with-
                out discrimination on the basis of sex.
                (Sec.143.422.2.) Discrimination on the basis of
                sex and sexual harassment are against the pub-
                lic policy of North Carolina.

Remedies: Appropriate affirmative relief.

Agency: Human Relations Council
                16 Church St. N.E.
                Concord, N.C. 28025
                704-795-3537

Website: http://www.oah.state.nc.us/civil/

NORTH DAKOTA

Law: North Dakota Century Code Annotated Sections 14-02.4-01 to 14-02.4-21. North Dakota Fair Employment Practices Act.

Scope: Employers, employment agencies, labor organizations, but not employers with employees for less than one-quarter of a year, domestic and certain family workers and political staff. (Secs. 14-02.4-03, 14-02.4-02, 14-02.4-10.)

Covers: It is a discriminatory practice for an employer to fail or refuse to hire a person or to discharge an employee or to accord adverse or unequal treatment to a person or employee with respect to application, hiring, training, apprenticeship, tenure, promotion, upgrading, compensation, layoff, or a term, privilege or condition of employment because of sex, unless due to a bona fide occupational qualification reasonably necessary to the normal operation of that particular business. (Sec. 14-02.4-03, 14-02.4-08.) Specifically makes sexual harassment a form of sex discrimination. Defines sexual harassment as: unwelcome sexual advances, requests for sexual favors, sexually motivated physical conduct or other verbal or physical conduct or communication of a sexual nature when: (a) submission to that conduct is made a term or condition, either explicitly or implicitly, of obtaining employment; (b) submission to or

(continued)

rejection of that conduct or communication by an individual is used as a factor in decisions affecting that individual's employment; or (c) that conduct or communication has the purpose or effect of substantially interfering with an individual's employment. (Sec. 14-02.4-02.(5).)

Remedies: Back pay (from which interim earnings are deducted), temporary relief orders, attorney fees (prevailing party), other appropriate relief.

Agency: Division of Human Rights
600 East Boulevard Ave., Dept. 406
Bismark, North Dakota 58505-0340
800-582-8032

Website: http://www.state.nd.us/labor/

OHIO

Law: Page's Ohio Revised Code Annotated, Sections 4112.01-.99. Ohio Fair Employment Practices Law

Scope: Public and private employers, employment agencies, labor organizations, but not employers with less than four workers, domestic workers. (Secs. 4112.01, 4112.02.)

Covers: It is an unlawful discriminatory practice for an employer, because of sex, to discharge without cause, to refuse to hire or otherwise to discriminate against that person with respect to hire, tenure, terms, conditions or privileges of employment or in any matter directly or indirectly related to employment unless based on a bona fide occupational qualification. (Sec.4112.02(A),(E).)

Remedies: Hiring, reinstatement, promotion, back pay (from which interim earnings may be deducted), cease and desist orders, other appropriate relief.

Agency: Ohio Civil Rights Commission
Akron Regional Office
Akron Government Building - Suite 205
161 South High Street
Akron, Ohio 44308
330-643-3100
TTY 330-643-3100

Cincinnati Regional Office
Holiday Office Park
801-B West 8th Street, 2nd Floor,
Cincinnati, Ohio 45203
513-852-3344
TTY 513-852-3344

Cleveland Regional Office
885 Lausche State Office Building
615 West Superior Avenue, 8th Floor
Cleveland, Ohio 44113
216-787-3150
TTY 216-787-3150

Columbus Regional Office
1111 East Broad Street Suite 301
Columbus, Ohio 43205
614-466-5928
TTY 614-752-2391

Dayton Regional Office
800 Miami Valley Tower
40 West 4th Street, Suite 800
Dayton, Ohio 45402
937-285-6500
TTY 937-285-6500

Toledo Regional Office
One Government Center - Suite 936
Jackson and Erie Streets
Toledo, Ohio 43604
419-245-2900
TTY 419-245-2900

Website: http://www.state.oh.us/crc/

OKLAHOMA

Law: Oklahoma Statutes Annotated, Title 25, Section 1101-1802. Oklahoma Civil Rights Act.

Scope: Public and private employers, employment agencies, labor organizations, but not employers with less than fifteen workers, domestic and certain family workers, nonprofit membership clubs. (Secs. 1301, 1302.)

Covers: It is an unlawful discriminatory practice for an employer to refuse to hire to discharge or otherwise to discriminate against an individual with respect to compensation, or the terms, conditions, privileges or responsibilities of employment because of sex, unless related to a bona fide occupational qualification which is reasonably necessary to the normal operations of the employer's business. (Sec.1302(A)(1).)

Remedies: Hiring, reinstatement, promotion, back pay (from which interim earnings are deducted), cease and desist orders, attorney fees under certain circumstances, other appropriate relief.

Agency: Oklahoma Human Rights Commission
              Jim Thorpe Building, Room 480
              2101 North Lincoln Boulevard
              Oklahoma City, Oklahoma 73105
              405-521-2360
              TDD 405-522-3993

(continued)

Tulsa Field Office
State Office Building, Room 302
440 South Houston
Tulsa, Oklahoma 74127
918-581-2733

Website: http://www.onenet.net/

OREGON

Law: Oregon Revised Statutes Annotated,
                Section 659.010 to 659.990.
                Oregon Fair Employment Practices Act.

Scope: Public and private employers, employment
                agencies, labor organizations, but not domestic
                or certain family workers.
                (Secs. 659.010, 659.030.)

Covers: It is an unlawful employment practice for an
                employer, because of sex, to refuse to hire or
                employ or to bar or discharge from employ-
                ment such individual unless related to a bona
                fide occupational qualification which is reason-
                ably necessary to the normal operations of the
                employer's business. (Sec. 659.030(1)(a).)

Remedies: Hiring, reinstatement, promotion, back pay,
                cease and desist orders, temporary relief
                orders, attorney fees to prevailing party, other
                appropriate relief.

Agency: Oregon Civil Rights Division
                Bureau of Labor and Industry
                800 NE Oregon Street
                Portland, OR 97232
                English: 503-731-4075
                Spanish: 503-373-1434

Website: http://www.boli.state.or.us/civil/

PENNSYLVANIA

Law: Purdon's Pennsylvania Consolidated Statutes Annotated, Title 43, Sections 951- 955.

Scope: Public and private employers, employment agencies, labor organizations, but not employers with less than four workers, domestic or certain family workers, religious organizations, or agricultural workers. (Secs. 954, 955.)

Covers: It is an unlawful discriminatory practice, unless based upon a bona fide occupational qualification, for an employer, because of sex, to refuse to hire or employ or to bar or to discharge from employment or otherwise to discriminate against such individual with respect to compensation, hire, tenure, terms, conditions, privileges of employment if that person is able and competent to perform the services required. (Sec.955(a).) There are specific guidelines on sexual harassment which define how the human rights commission defines and investigates sexual harassment cases. (Human Relations Commission Guidelines on Sexual Harassment, 11 Pa.bull.No.5 (Jan. 31, 1981).)

Remedies: Hiring, reinstatement, promotion, back pay, cease and desist orders, attorney fees to prevailing party if case goes to court, other appropriate relief.

(continued)

Agency: Pennsylvania Human Relations Commission
101 South Second Street - Suite 300
Harrisburg, PA 17105-3145
717-787-4410
TTY 717-783-9308

Website: http://www.phrc.state.pa.us/

RHODE ISLAND

Law: General laws of Rhode Island,
            Sections 28-5-1 to 28-5-39.

Scope: Public and private employers, employment
            agencies, labor organizations, but not employers
            with less than four workers, domestic and cer-
            tain family workers. (Secs. 28-5-6, 28-5-7.)

Covers: It is an unlawful employment practice for an
            employer to refuse to hire any applicant
            because of sex or to discharge or discriminate
            against an employee with respect to hire,
            tenure, compensation, terms, conditions or
            privileges of employment, or any other matter
            directly or indirectly related to employment.
            (Sec. 28-5-7(1)(i).)

Remedies: Hiring, reinstatement, promotion, back pay
            (including all raises and benefits to which the
            employee would have been entitled), cease and
            desist orders, temporary restraining orders,
            money damages, attorney fees to prevailing
            plaintiffs, other appropriate relief.

Agency: Rhode Island Commission for Human Rights
            10 Abbott Park Place
            Providence, Rhode Island 02903-3768
            401-222-2661
            TDD 401-222-2664

Website: http://www.state.ri.us/

SOUTH CAROLINA

Law: Code of Laws of South Carolina
Sections 1-13-10 to 1-13-100.

Scope: Employers, employment agencies, labor organizations, but not employers with less than fifteen workers, public officials' staff, social membership clubs. (Secs. 1-13.30, 1-13-80.)

Covers: It is an unlawful employment practice for an employer to fail or refuse to hire, bar, discharge from employment or otherwise discriminate against an individual with respect to compensation, or terms, conditions or privileges of employment because of sex, unless related to a bona fide occupational qualification which is reasonably necessary to the normal operations of the employer's business.
(Sec.1302(A)(1), (I)(1).)

Remedies: Hiring, reinstatement, promotion, back pay (from which interim earnings are deducted), cease and desist orders, temporary restraining orders, attorney fees, other appropriate relief.

Agency: South Carolina Human Affairs Commission
Post Office Box 4490
2611 Forest Drive, Suite 200,
Columbia, SC 29204
800-521-0725
TDD 803-253-4125

Website: http://www.state.sc.us/schac/

SOUTH DAKOTA

Law: South Dakota Codified Laws Annotated,
            Sections 20-13-1 to 20-13-56.
            South Dakota Human Relations Act.

Scope: Public and private employers, employment
            agencies, labor organizations.
            (Secs. 20-13-10—20-13-12.)

Covers: It is an unfair or discriminatory practice for any
            person, because of sex to fail or refuse to hire,
            to discharge or accord adverse or unequal treat-
            ment to any person or employee with respect
            to application, hiring, training, apprenticeship,
            tenure, promotion, upgrading, compensation,
            layoff or any term or condition of employment.
            (Sec. 20-13-10.)

Remedies: Hiring, reinstatement, promotion, back pay,
            cease and desist orders, other appropriate relief.

Agency: South Dakota Division of Human Rights
            118 West Capitol Avenue
            Pierre, South Dakota 57501
            605-773-4493

Website: http://www.state.sd.us/dcr/hr/

TENNESSEE

Law: Tennessee Code Annotated,
Sections 4-21-101 to 4-21-408.
Tennessee Fair Employment Practices Law.

Scope: Public and private employers, employment
agencies, labor organizations, but not employers
with less than eight workers, domestic or certain family workers. (Secs. 4-21-102, 4-21-401.)

Covers: It is a discriminatory practice for an employer
to fail or refuse to hire or discharge or otherwise to discriminate against an individual with
respect to compensation, terms, conditions or
privileges of employment because of sex, unless
based on a bona fide occupational qualification
that is reasonably necessary to the normal operation of that particular business.
(Sec.4-21-401, 4-21-406.)

Remedies: Hiring, reinstatement, promotion, back pay
(from which interim earnings are deducted),
cease and desist orders, temporary relief and
restraining orders, money damages, attorney
fees, other appropriate relief.

Agency: Tennessee Human Rights Commission
170 North Main Street
State Office Building
Memphis, TN 38103
901-543-7389

Website: http://www.state.tn.us/humanrights/

TEXAS

Law: Vernon's Texas Codes Annotated, Labor Code Section 21.001 -21.051. Texas Commission on Human Rights Act.

Scope: Public and private employers, employment agencies, labor organizations, but not employers with less than fifteen workers, certain family workers, political staff or statewide hometown plan staff. (Secs. 21.051-.053, 21.002, 21.117, 21.118.)

Covers: An employer commits an unlawful employment practice if, because of sex, the employer fails or refuses to hire an individual, discharges an individual or discriminates in any other manner against an individual in connection with compensation, or the terms, conditions or privileges of employment, unless related to a bona fide occupational qualification which is reasonably necessary to the normal operations of the employer's business. (Sec. 21.051.) Requires sexual harassment training for state employees. (Sec. 21.010.)

Remedies: Hiring, reinstatement, promotion, back pay (from which interim earnings are deducted), temporary relief and restraining orders, attorney fees to prevailing party, other appropriate relief.

(continued)

Agency: Texas Commission on Human Rights
6330 Highway 290 East, Suite 250
Austin, TX 78723
512-437-3450

Website: http://www.state.tx.us/

UTAH

Law: Utah Code Annotated,
            Sections 34A-5-101 to 108.
            Utah Antidiscrimination Act.

Scope: Public and private employers, employment
            agencies, labor organizations, but not employers
            with less than 15 workers, religious organiza-
            tions. (Secs. 34A-5-102.)

Covers: An employer may not refuse to hire, promote,
            discharge, demote, or terminate any person, or
            to retaliate against, harass, or discriminate in
            matters of compensation or in terms, privileges,
            and conditions of employment against any per-
            son otherwise qualified, because of sex unless
            based on a bona fide occupational qualification.
            (Sec. 34A-5-106.)

Remedies: Reinstatement, back pay, benefits, cease and
            desist orders, attorney fees to prevailing plaintiff,
            other appropriate relief.

Agency: Utah Antidiscrimination and Labor Division
            160 East 300 South, 3rd Floor
            Salt Lake City, UT 84111
            Mailing: P.O. Box 146630
            Salt Lake City, UT 84114-6630
            800-222-1238
            TDD 801-530-7685

Website: http://www.labor.state.ut.us/

VERMONT

Law: Vermont Statutes Annotated, Title 21,
Sections 495, 495g.
Vermont Fair Employment Practices Act.

Scope: Public and private employers, employment
agencies, labor organizations, but not labor
organizations that represent less than five
workers. (Secs. 495, 495d.)

Covers: It is an unlawful employment practice, except
on the basis of a bona fide occupational qualification, for any employer to discriminate against
any individual because of sex. (Sec. 495.)
Sexual harassment is specifically covered as a
form of sex discrimination and means unwelcome sexual advances, requests for sexual
favors, and other verbal or physical conduct of
a sexual nature when: (a) submission to that
conduct is made either explicitly or implicitly a
term or condition of employment; or (b) submission to or rejection of such conduct by an
individual is used as a component of the basis
for employment decisions affecting that individual; or (c) the conduct has the purpose or
effect of substantially interfering with an individual's work performance or creating an
intimidating, hostile or offensive work environment. (Sec. 495d.)

(continued)

Remedies: Reinstatement, restitution of wages or benefits, injunction, damages, attorney fees, other appropriate relief.

Agency: Vermont Human Rights Commission
135 State Street, Drawer 33
Montpelier, VT 05633-6301
802-828-2480

Website: http://www.state.vt.us/atg/

VIRGINIA

Law: Annotated Code of Virginia, Sections 2.2-3900 to 2.2-3902. Virginia Human Rights Act.

Scope: State, its contractors and subcontractors with contracts of at least $10,000. (Secs. 15.2-1604, 2.2-4200-4311.)

Covers: An unlawful discriminatory practice is conduct that violates any Virginia or federal statute or regulation governing discrimination on the basis of sex. (Sec. 2.2-3901.)

Remedies: Not specified, but back pay and other appropriate affirmative relief can be awarded.

Agency: Council on Human Rights
Suite 1202, Washington Building
1100 Bank Street
Richmond, Virginia 23219
804-225-2292

Website: http://www.state.va.us/

WASHINGTON

Law: West's Revised Code of Washington Annotated. Sections 49.60.010 to 49.60.320. Washington Law Against Discrimination.

Scope: Public and private employers, employment agencies, labor organizations, but not employers with less than eight workers, domestic and certain family workers, religious or nonprofit organizations. (Secs. 49.60.040, 49.60.180.200.)

Covers: The right to be free from discrimination because of sex is recognized as and declared to be a civil right. The right includes the right to obtain and hold employment without discrimination. (Sec. 49.60.030.) It is an unfair practice for any employer to refuse to hire any person because of sex, unless based upon a bona fide occupational qualification, or to discharge or bar any person from employment because of sex or to discriminate against any person in compensation or in other terms or conditions of employment because of sex. (Sec.49.60.180.)

Remedies: Hiring, reinstatement, promotion, back pay, cease and desist orders, temporary relief or restraining orders, attorney fees to prevailing plaintiffs (or defendants if case brought in bad faith), other appropriate relief.

(continued)

Agency: Washington State Human Rights Commission
              Seattle District Office
              Melbourne Tower, #921
              1511 Third Avenue
              Seattle, WA 98101-1626
              800-605-7324
              TTY 206-587-5168

Website: http://www.wa.gov/hrc/

WEST VIRGINIA

Law: West Virginia Code,
Sections 5-11-1 to 5-11-19.
West Virginia Human Rights Act.

Scope: Public and private employers, employment
agencies, labor organizations, but not employers
with less than twelve workers, domestic and
certain family workers, private clubs.
(Secs. 5-11-3.)

Covers: Equal opportunity in employment is hereby
declared to be a human right or civil right of all
persons without regard to sex. (Sec.5-11-2.) It
shall be an unlawful discriminatory practice,
unless based upon a bona fide occupational
qualification, or except where based upon
applicable security regulations established by
the United States or the state of West Virginia
or its agencies or political subdivisions, for any
employer to discriminate against an individual
with respect to compensation, hire, tenure,
terms, conditions or privileges of employment
if the individual is able and competent to perform the services required. (Sec. 5-11-9.)

Remedies: Hiring, reinstatement, promotion, back pay,
cease and desist orders, attorney fees to prevailing plaintiff if case goes to court, other appropriate relief.

(continued)

Agency: State of West Virginia Human Rights
            Commission 1321 Plaza East Room 108A
            Charleston, WV 25301
            304-558-2616 or 1-888-676-5546
            TDD 304-558-0085

Website: http://www.state.wv.us/wvhrc/

WISCONSIN

Law: West's Wisconsin Statutes Annotated,
Sections 111.36(1)(b).

Scope: Public and private employers, employment
agencies, labor organizations, but not certain
family employers. (Secs. 111.32, 111.325.)

Covers: It is an act of employment discrimination to
refuse to hire, employ, admit or license any
individual, to bar or terminate from employment or labor organization membership any
individual, or to discriminate against any individual in promotion, compensation or in terms,
conditions or privileges of employment or labor
organization membership because of sex.
(Sec.111.322, 111.321.) Unless based on a
bona fide occupational qualification, sex discrimination includes engaging in sexual harassment, or implicitly or explicitly making or permitting acquiescence in or submission to sexual
harassment a term or condition of employment; or making or permitting acquiescence in,
submission to or rejection of sexual harassment
the basis or any part of the basis for any
employment decision affecting an employee,
other than an employment decision that is disciplinary action against an employee for engaging in sexual harassment in violation of this
paragraph; or permitting sexual harassment to
have the purpose or effect of substantially

(continued)

interfering with an employees work performance or of creating an intimidating, hostile or offensive work environment.

Sexual harassment also consists of unwelcome verbal or physical conduct directed at another individual because of that individuals gender and that has the purpose or effect of creating an intimidating, hostile or offensive work environment or has the purpose or effect of substantially interfering with that individuals work performance. Substantial interference with an employees work performance or creation of an intimidating, hostile or offensive work environment is established when the conduct is such that a reasonable person under the same circumstances as the employee would consider the conduct sufficiently severe or pervasive to interfere substantially with the persons work performance or to create an intimidating, hostile or offensive work environment. (Sec.1136.)

Remedies: Appropriate relief, back pay (from which interim earnings are deducted).

Agency: Wisconsin Equal Rights Division
201 East Washington, Ave.
P.O. Box 8928
Madison, Wisconsin 53708
608-266-7552 or 608-266-1997

Website: http://www.dwd.state.wi.us/er/

WYOMING

Law: Wyoming Statutes Annotated §§ 27-9-101 to
              27-9-108. Wyoming Fair Employment Practices
              Act.

Scope: Public and private employers, employment
              agencies, labor organizations, but not employers
              with less than 2 workers, religious organiza-
              tions. §§ 27-9-102.

Covers: It is a discriminatory or unfair employment
              practice for an employer to refuse to hire, to
              discharge, to promote or demote, or to discrim-
              inate in matters of compensation or the terms,
              conditions or privileges of employment against,
              a qualified disabled person or any person other-
              wise qualified, because of sex. §27-9-105.

Remedies: Hiring, reinstatement, promotion, back pay,
              cease and desist orders, other appropriate relief.

Agency: Wyoming Fair Employment Division
              US West Building
              6101 Yellowstone, Rm. 259c
              Cheyenne, Wyoming 82002
              307-777-7261

Website: http://www.state.wy.us/

INDEX

W

Z

ABOUT THE AUTHOR

Mary L. Boland received her law degree from John Marshall Law School. A long-time victim's advocate, she has worked to pass legislation protecting victim's rights and has served as a consultant to various federal agencies. She is currently the chair of the Victim's Committee of the Criminal Justice Section of the American Bar Association and co-chair of the Victims Issues Committee of the Prosecutor's Bar Association of Illinois. Ms. Boland is a full-time prosecutor and an adjunct faculty member of Roosevelt University in Chicago, Illinois.